TRAVELS IN LANGUEDOC

Secrets to a Memorable Visit

Salut, Andrea.

Andrea Swan with Monique Guezel

Suite 300 – 990 Fort Street
Victoria, BC, Canada V8V 3K2
www.friesenpress.com

ISBN
978-1-4602-5465-3 (Hardcover)
978-1-4602-5466-0 (Paperback)
978-1-4602-5467-7 (eBook)

1. Cooking, Regional & Ethnic, French

Distributed to the trade by The Ingram Book Company

TABLE OF CONTENTS

"The traveler is active: he went strenuously in search of people, of adventure, of experience. The tourist is passive: he expects interesting things to happen to him. He goes 'sight-seeing'"-
Daniel J. Boorstein, b 1919, American Writert

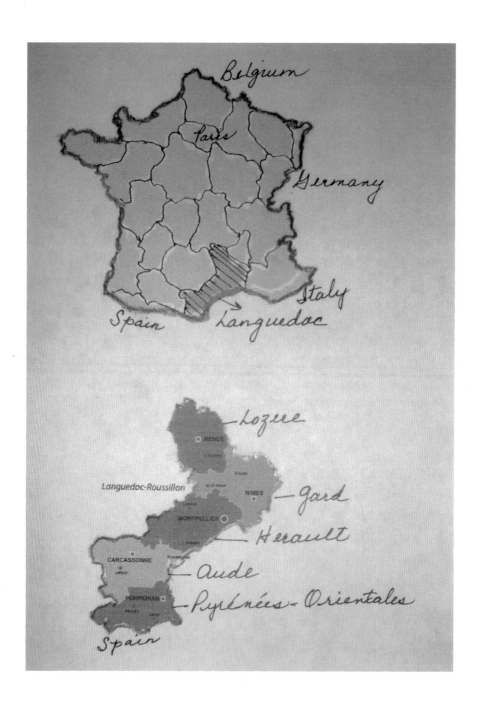

Andrea Swan with Monique Guezel

France is divided into 22 regional districts that are then subdivided into 96 departments. Languedoc is officially called Languedoc-Rousillon and is made up of the five departments of Pyrenees-Orientale, Aude, Herault, Gard and Lozere. The total population of the region is about 2.5 million people. While French is the official language of the region, there is a resurgence in the original dialect of Occitan. Montpellier is the capital of the region with each department having a *sous-prefecture* (sub-capital). Other major cities include Beziers, Narbonne, Carcassonne, Nîmes and Perpignan.

While it covers only 10,000 square miles, Languedoc is geographically very diverse with the Pyrenées and the Cevennes bordering the west and northeast boundaries. Broad river valleys carved by the Aude, Herault and Rhone rivers provide exceptionally rich agricultural land. The two hundred kilometers of beach along the Mediterranean ensure a temperate climate.

INTRODUCTION

It has been ten years since my husband and I bought a house in a small village in Languedoc and Monique Guezel came into our lives. Since then, we have shared our house and village with many people and Monique has provided the insights, little known stories and special hidden treasures that can make any holiday special. Monique was born in the region and has lived here all her life. Her knowledge and love of the area are evident in her stories, cooking and savoirfaire. More importantly, she has opened doors, provided wise counsel and generously shared her knowledge of the region and her recipes that reflect age-old traditions and secrets of Languedoc. "Monique says" has become our mantra to change a vacation in Languedoc from a holiday to a memorable experience.

The book is written as a monthly guide to the region. Each month Monique and I introduce you to key foods and activities, provide background to specific customs, traditions and places and end with recipes that are special for the month. Along with the recipes, come Monique's comments on the "correct" way to prepare each recipe. By the time you have read the information, the recipes and the anecdotes that we share, you will be able to best answer your question "What is the best time for us to visit Languedoc?"

Monique and I hope that as you read through the pages, you learn from our information, our stories and from "Monique says". For those of you who are contemplating a stay in

Languedoc and want to maximize your visit, we hope that this book will provide you with the answers you are looking for and make your "*temps retrouvé*" (time found) a delight. Whether you are coming for a week or longer, there are ample opportunities to immerse yourself in this fascinating region of France and to take advantage of "Monique says".

We have enjoyed the help of many friends and family in writing this book. They have shared stories, offered suggestions, tested recipes and kindly aided in editing our writing. We thank them all. My French friend, Jacky Ingram gets the credit for the cover artwork. All other images are Andrea's. We also want to thank the people at FreisenPress, especially Christine Whiteside, for their help and expertise in bringing this book from manuscript to the finished product. Monique and I especially wish to thank our husbands, Pierre and Andy for their support and comments in writing this book and sharing our lives in France.

JANUARY

Greek & Roman history, bisous, les soldes,
truffles, wine, market shopping

January in Languedoc conjures up images of wood fires burning steadily, walks in the afternoon sunshine, greeting friends at the markets and a slower pace of living. Visiting now would be perfect for those who are interested in a quiet, laid back holiday, in learning more about the regions people on an intimate level, designing their own tours and who have a reasonable fluency in French to navigate newspapers and conversations. There are enormous opportunities to immerse oneself in various aspects of life in Languedoc. Given the possibilities, it is probably best to identify one or two particular areas of interest and focus on those. This can be as wide-ranging as Greek or Roman history, the beaches, Cathar history, wines or foods of the region, pilgrimage routes, local markets, feasts and festivals, sports, and fashion.

∞

The southern Languedoc was a stopping place for both Greek and Roman armies. The museum in Narbonne houses a large display of artifacts including the remains of a Roman road that is open for today's travelers to walk along (however, it is a very short example). A visit to the large Sunday morning market followed by lunch and a museum visit is a great all-encompassing day trip. The remnants of the Via Dometia, the ancient Roman highway from Spain to Italy ran through much of the southern Languedoc and there are still vestiges of it in towns and villages. Languedoc tourist bureaus provide extensive materials for developing a self-guided tour and as many of the archeological sites are in the open, it can be a January focus of your visit.

> After lunch in a seaside restaurant in Agde, we headed to the nearby museum "L'Ephebe" to check out their artifacts. This small museum is located near Cap d'Agde and houses numerous examples of Greek and Roman items excavated from the Agde waterways. It was quiet and the hosts were happy to answer our numerous questions. It felt as though we were being given our own private tour back through history. What we consider as antiquity, most local people consider

part of their everyday life. The *Pont Roman* in St Thibery is one such example. It's an easy bike ride on a sunny afternoon from any of the surrounding villages and offers a chance to wonder what life was like back in Medieval and Roman times.

No trip to the eastern Languedoc region is complete without seeing the Pont du Gard, the Roman aqueduct that supplied water to the city of Nîmes. While it has been fully restored, one still marvels at the feat of construction undertaken by the Romans centuries ago. Walking under, over or beside it, one can't help but wonder how they figured out the construction techniques and moved the mass of rocks without benefit of modern cranes and bulldozers. The interpretation centre provides excellent background material as well as modern conveniences of lunch and gift shops. The route to the Pont du Gard, passes through the city of Nîmes where a visit will add to the understanding and appreciation of the realities of Roman life. While the Roman arena and temple to Diana have been updated to serve the needs of the current Nimoise, it is easy to see how the people of the time simply incorporated previous cut stones and foundations into their buildings. It's such a different approach to life in North America where bulldozers make way for 'new and improved'. In France, wherever you look in the old towns and villages there are vestiges of a previous civilization peeking out amidst the current dwellings. In our own house, we often wonder if the large square, hand hewn stones that make up the outer walls were previously part of some Roman structures.

∞

While swimming in the Mediterranean is not likely except for the hardiest of souls or the New Years ritual, walking on the long sandy beaches in full sunshine and then enjoying a drink at a seaside café is a wonderful way to pass an afternoon. Languedoc, with over 200KM of sandy beaches stretching from Montpellier to the Spanish border, offers a pleasant escape on a sunny afternoon in January. There are numerous villages along the way that have wonderful opportunities for exploration. Even in January, some of the local restaurants are open and feature a wide range of seafood. Locally harvested oysters and mussels are a staple in this area and can be enjoyed at most restaurants. Many of the fish varieties come from the Mediterranean and the markets will feature daily catches.

> As the folks back home were shoveling snow, we were strolling along the beach at Sete, a light wind providing enough challenge for the local paragliders. There was no need for us to bundle up-a sweater and jacket did the trick-however, sunglasses were a necessity. It was Saturday afternoon about 3PM and the strollers seemed to be suggesting by their slow gait that this was the time to take the post siesta exercise; families, couples and teenagers all exhibited a pleasure in being out in the warm January sunshine.

∞

In France, each month features special feasts and festivals commemorating religious events or more commonly, the celebration of the land and sea and their gifts. January 6th marks Epiphany and the featured dish is the *Galette du Roi* (king's cake). This circular puffed pastry confection is filled with *frangipani* (almond flavoured custard) and contains a *fève* (little figurine) hidden in it. The person who finds the prize gets to wear the crown and be king or queen for the day. These cakes are available in all patisseries throughout France and usually have a "crown" sold with them. Different regions will fill or decorate the cake with local variations.

> We had missed buying our baguette for lunch and stopped in a nearby village to check out their wares. The boulangerie window had been transformed into a dense array of miniature fèves for the Galette du Roi. I had never seen such possibilities as there were in this window-along with the traditional religious galette figures, one could even purchase a family of Smurfs, various fairy tale characters or even a variety of animals.

∞

Visitors often remark about the friendliness of people in Languedoc. With just a few words of French, you will see people welcome you and attempt to engage you in conversation. One particular habit that is prevalent throughout France is exchanging *bisous* (welcome kisses) when meeting someone. It can be confusing for a visitor to figure out the *politesse* (politeness) of the procedure. Which side does one start on; how many kisses to give; does one kiss the cheek?

Monique explained the niceties of the bisous greeting to me and even she does some second-guessing sometimes. In Languedoc, the usual habit is, moving towards the persons' left, you touch each other's left cheek and make a kissing sound then repeat on the other side. One never actually kisses the cheek. In the coastal villages, three kisses are given, beginning towards the left while in the north it's four kisses. She remarked that she still is on guard for that extra movement to initiate an additional kiss or to make sure she isn't about to bump the other person's nose. So if you are greeted with a bisous, enjoy it and laugh if your noses colli

In Languedoc, January is the time for the *Festival des Truffes*. This does not refer to those melt-in-your-mouth chocolates but to a smelly, black ball dug up typically by a dog or pig. Truffles are the kings of mushrooms, can be worth more than many good bottles of wine and enjoy their own mystique and lore. Truffles qualify for their own festivals and in Languedoc there are two well-known ones in January. Uzès, in the Gard, holds its festival on the second Sunday of January while the Clermont-Herault festival is on the last Sunday in January.

Today was the Truffle Festival! We headed out early for the Clermont-l'Herault festival in order to beat the rush and see the special processions that often accompany such events. As we entered the town, we were surprised to see few people and quickly discovered that the newspaper information was incorrect-we were one week early. As Peter Mayle would write, "normalement"… However, after all, this is Sunday morning in France and the other typical activity is to go out into the countryside, to connect with ones *patrimonie* (history and culture). So off we went, following the smaller "D" roads and meandering through hill and dale into tiny hamlets of only a handful of people. The light caught the variations in the stone houses, outlining how and where additions were made over the ages.

After winding our way along a series of single track, hairpin curves we were awarded with panoramic views. The scene was spectacular as we looked out over the valley and across to the hills of the *Montagne Noire*. We did not dare linger as the reality of the one-car road set in but we promised ourselves we would retrace our route and explore these hidden treasures more fully. Eventually, using our detailed map, we came to a small village and found a restaurant open that featured an excellent *formule* (daily special) for $30.00 each. After two hours of savouring the local wine, terrine, main course of duck and then homemade desserts, we headed off towards home. In keeping with the surprises so far, we took a sharp right-hand turn towards a small sign indicating the remains of a ninth century abbey. The Fontfroide Abbey was only open from 2-4 on Sundays in January so again, we lucked out as we ventured into another unexpected treat. Recent renovations and information developed by a dedicated group of local volunteers provided us with a glimpse of an important historical part of French life. We noticed that the other couple visiting the chapel had an English guidebook like ours; on hearing us, they initiated a discussion that led to the discovery that they were from England and planning a trip to North America the following September and would be visiting our city. Throughout Languedoc, it is easy to strike up conversations with people, regardless of nationality, and so often one finds examples of these "small world" stories.

In the quiet days of January, experiences such as these are a frequent part of life here—the unexpected, the mysterious, the memorable. The following Sunday, we again made our way to Clermont-l'Herault and this time found ourselves in the mist of the Truffle Festival that had expanded into a regional food fair. We ran the gauntlet of an array of foods, wines and product samples from the region. We sampled various fresh cheeses from the Larzac area north of Clermont-l'Herault, aligot, the traditional potato and cheese dish of Lozere, being prepared in huge cauldrons, local apples and quince varieties that never appear in the supermarkets, the tastiest spice cakes, locally made nougat with almonds and hazelnuts from the families' trees. And of course, TRUFFLES- black, woody balls about the size of golf balls costing 900E per kilo ($450/lb) each. Granted, one only needs a small shaving to change a simple omelet or risotto into something quite divine. The trick with truffles is knowing what you are buying-judging from the people hovering around the various truffle merchants, it seemed obvious that these people knew how to judge a truffle and the truffle sellers. One merchant had numerous prospective buyers who clearly were intent on examining his product and ensuring that they were not being tricked while another had no takers- a good indicator of truffle-buying expertise. Even if you don't purchase anything, as a visitor, the experience of watching the interactions is worth the adventure. Are truffles worth the mystery-a friend tells the story of wandering into a village up in the hills one Sunday morning and coming across the local truffle festival. He purchased three small truffles and carefully wrapped and re-wrapped them to hide their powerful, earthy smell. As he described the simple truffle omelette that he prepared the evening I think it safe to say that it was worth it.

∞

Languedoc is the largest grape-growing region in France and is now focusing on improving the quality rather than the quantity of its wines. As a result, it offers both the novice and expert wine lover a chance to discover secret treasures. The regional government has recently updated the legislation that governs wine labeling and new Languedoc *appellations* (regional designations) are coming into being. The AOC (appellation d'origine controlee) French system of wine labeling and production is different from most of the rest of the world. In the current North American market, many wines are typically produced and sold according to the grape variety-Chardonnay, Merlot, Cabernet, Syrah. This means that the bottle must contain at least 75% of that grape. However, the wine can be made from grapes that come from a variety of regions. This allows winemakers to produce more consistent wines year after year to ensure good market control. In France the "Appellation AOC" system legislates that the grapes must come from a specific area that is best suited for the grapes-Bordeaux, Cote de Rhones, Bourgogne, Chablis. This means that all the grapes must come from the region, although there can be a variety of grapes used in a specific wine. The more restricted the *Appellation AOC* designation, the smaller the area allocated for the grape gathering and the wine-making- a *Vin de Pays D'Oc* means that the grapes will come from anywhere in Languedoc and typically represent a lower cost wine; a *Vin de Caux* means that the grapes can come only from specific fields around the village of Caux. Some may even be restricted to a particular Chateau or Domaine. This can result in greater difficulty producing a good wine as the wine-maker will be at the mercy of the ever-changing annual growing conditions. It is this approach that reflects the idea of the French wines being *terroir* wines-they reflect more accurately from year to year the subtle variations of the weather, soil and micro-climate of the region. Wine discoveries can happen even in January as *caves* (vineyard wine shop) are frequently open during the winter months and offer an opportunity for more personal attention. It's easy to drive around and spot *ouvert* (open) signs along the various side roads and villages. In our village alone AOC Cotes de Thongue, we are surrounded by 45 domaines, individual wine-makers producing wine from their own terroir. Several well-known appellation regions in Languedoc include St Chinian, Faugères, PicPoul, Corbieres, Minervois, Clairette, Muscat and La Clape. This means that there will be numerous winegrowers within each of these appellations, each eager to share their stories and their products. Many of these producers have lived and worked in Languedoc for generations but there is a new breed of winemaker-those who have come to Languedoc for a visit, fallen in love with the region and turned their back on careers and lives in other countries to immerse themselves in the struggles of the land. Some are making a living and some are thriving but all tell a story of hard work, commitment and love of the land. January offers the chance to meet and engage with these *vignerons* (grape grower who makes his/her own wine) in a relaxed, intimate way. To learn more, an excellent website is "languedoc-wine".

My husband and I set out on a warm sunny, Tuesday afternoon to visit two nearby vineyards whose wine we particularly enjoy. Madame Wyss came from Switzerland in the 1980s for a short visit to friends who lived in Languedoc. She and her husband were so enamored by the region, the climate and the possibilities that they left behind mid-life careers and settled in a small village in Languedoc. Over a glass of wine, she shares with us her story of the slow, hard work of rebuilding a ruin, re-establishing the vines and ultimately, producing award winning wines. It is warm in the January sunshine as we visit with her. Her obvious deep love for this adopted land is evident as she described which vines the grapes come from, how they are harvested and what "green" techniques she uses to protect the land and the wine. She is passionate about the need to respect the elements and work with the natural conditions of the land in order to release the potential each year in creating the new wine. This is not about seeking consistency in a product but about engaging in a transformative practice. As we talked with her, we sensed that there is a spiritual component to her story, similar to the experience we have had with other winemakers.

On another venture, Monique and I came upon the tiny hamlet of Notre Dame de Mougères with one large building, a twelveth century monastery that has been re-opened and updated. The cloistered order of Catholic nuns now occupying the monastery opens their gift shop to display their handmade icons and carvings. The history of this monastery is similar to others found across France-destroyed during the Revolution, bought up by locals for a song, left to fall into ruin over the generations but now being reclaimed by a new group aspiring to the same ideals as their ancestors. The religious sisters again offer up the practices of the past-contemplative practice, hospitality to others or service to the community. The restored chapel provided evidence of its previous focus as a pilgrim's stop. The nun explained that the monastery had provided food and accommodation from the fourteenth century up to the Revolution and was again offering respite from the pressures of daily living through a renewed life as a retreat centre. Petit-Soeur Blanc spoke so gently and quietly that we had to listen closely so as not to miss a word of her clearly enunciated French. She explained how the sisters were a cloistered order and therefore, there was only one sister available to interact with the public. All the other sisters spent their time in silence within the cloister walls. In response to Monique's questions, she explained that the monastery and all the surrounding lands had been turned over to the Religious Order several years ago but that they were unable to manage the vineyards. We learned how they have adapted to changing times but remain committed to the monastic life. The vineyards surrounding the monastery have been cultivated since Roman times. Today, the vineyards and the winemaking is left up to a young, local family who have developed a livelihood by tapping into the potentially lucrative local wine producing market. There is a growing revival throughout Languedoc in this collaboration between the religious orders and vignerons. It is interesting how this centuries-old relationship has again emerged. In the past, it was often the monks themselves who cultivated the fields and produced the wine or other alcoholic beverages. The new, beautifully designed cave featured at least twelve varieties of whites, rosés and reds-all the grapes grown on the property as well as a variety of *produits de terroir* (products from their land) from the local area. The young man who spoke with us was the son of the vigneron. His family name is Saint-Exupery, a famous name in France and one closely aligned with the Catholic Church; there seemed to be a certain rightness in this twenty-first century collaboration. He explained how several of the grape varieties had been introduced from other wine producing areas of France because of the links between monasteries in centuries past. As a result, this small parcel of land was producing some unique and delightful wines that we, of course, sampled. The innumerable questions and patient responses ensured that we did not race through this afternoon experience but instead entered into an intimate experience of understanding the region, the values and the gifts. January is like that in Languedoc.

∞

January offers advantages as New Year celebrations and local festivities are still happening as part of the Christmas season. They are open to everyone in the village and if one is interested, it is easy to reserve a place at an event. It is a great way to mingle with the community and feel like you belong. Each village has an event where the mayor hosts a gathering to give his or her good wishes for the year to the townspeople. This always ends in with a *verre d'amitié*, (glass of wine) so it's a wonderful way to meet people in the local community. There will often be someone who speaks some English, whether they are from an English-speaking country or have learned English along the way. Regardless, one will be quickly welcomed into the group.

Delfina owned the local bar and was an enter-prising woman who constantly looked for ways to encourage business and bring people together in a January celebration. She was so excited as she described her newest idea-a supper club night with a local live band. The cost would be reason-able so that everyone could come. We assured her that our little band of Canadians would be there to join the party. We showed up at the appointed hour-at that time, we didn't realize that 30 minutes anytime after the appointed hour was still "on time". Of course, that made us the only arrivals and struck fear into us that this was going to be a small party. The crowds soon trickled in with much enthusiasm as friends found each other and chose their places. Delfina bounced from table to table greeting all those gathered and expressing her happiness at the community response to this new idea. Who could believe that so many people could get into the bar! As the drinks flowed, so too did the conversation and laughter. The band arrived just as food was being served and they set up in the far corner, quietly tuning their instruments. Betwcen courses, the music started-guitars, bass and keyboard. The soloist sang all the popular songs-and mostly in English. We had spoken to these people and they did not speak any English yet here they were, rattling off lyrics to well known English pop songs. The music was lively and meant to get people up dancing-there was an excess of females but that didn't bother anyone-as long as you were dancing it didn't matter who your partner was-young and old, male or female. We had earlier mentioned to Delfina that one of our party was an accomplished singer who regularly accompanied her husband's band. We knew something was up when we saw her whispering to the leader and looking our way. Before, we knew it, our friend, Vivienne was up on the stage getting her cues from the musicians. The crowd became so enthusiastic as she captured the rhythm of the music and belted out the words to "Mustang Sally". The placed rocked and an encore was called for. She duly obliged with "You Can Leave Your Hat On", helping forge French-Canadian relationships.

∞

France does have several large cities but the majority of the population lives in towns and villages of less than 30,000. The people are *paysans* (people of the land) and working the land continues to be evident, even in January. Many Parisians are known to say that even though they have lived in Paris for many years, they or their family are from a rural part of France; that is where the French heart is. Following a wonderful New Year's Eve celebration with Monique and her husband, Pierre, we walked out into the January 1st sunshine and meandered through the small roads surrounding our village. We saw the classic white vans so commonly used by workers throughout France. We watched a traditional New Year's Day event happening in field after field- father and sons out pruning the vines. Mothers and children gathered around the vehicles, talking and laughing. The New Year's celebration is a bigger family event than Christmas as families come from near and far to return to the family *terroir* (land). The pruning process continues throughout the coming months and in some villages, visitors can participate. The local *Mairie* (Town Hall) or tourist bureau has the names of vignerons who offer this opportunity or you could likely meet someone in the local bar and offer your help.

∞

January offers the possibility of creating your own tour of a region focusing on a personal interest. There is little that the region does not offer to both the novice and expert. France has an extensive walking trail system known as the Grand Randonées. These trails are well marked and are often based on pre-existing shepherds' tracks or farmers' trails. Local *tabacs* (tobacco stores that offer a range of items) sell the special randonées maps of each region and you would be well advised to purchase one before heading out on your own.

> After reading Black Dogs by Ian McEwan, a novel set in the Haute Languedoc, we were able to trace the journey taken by the characters. We could sense the characters' anxiety as we turned various corners on the route. We stopped in front of the Bergerie de Tedenat and gazed out over the landscape described so vividly by the author. On the trail, we met other walkers and came across a couple that was out gathering mushrooms. In a quintessentially French moment, all of these people entered into an animated conversation over the best way to prepare the mushrooms. Several of them quoted the recipes of their grandmothers as the definitive recipe! Such debate and such a wonderful afternoon

excursion guided by the brilliant writing of Ian McEwan.

∞

The Midi-Libre is the daily French newspaper of the Languedoc and is available at all tabacs, grocery stores and on line. It is your best source for information on what is happening in your area. Check out the Friday edition to see what special activities are happening over the weekend. If your French is rusty, the Languedoc does offer some resources to help you find your way. While this region does have fewer English speakers than other regions of France, there are a growing number of publications, clubs and Internet resources to help you. A couple of our favourites are BlaBlaBlah magazine, an English and French magazine published out of Pezenas and the Herault and Aude Times. They both offer good advice, current news of the region and a chance to connect with other English speakers. Their monthly calendars provide coverage of activities for much of the eastern Languedoc region.

∞

One special event that begins in mid-Jan and is quite foreign in North America and other European countries is *Les Soldes*. France legislates two annual sale periods each year-mid-January to early February and late-June to mid-July. The discounts start around 30% and drop weekly up to 80%, if anything is left. This law enables small shopkeepers to compete with the large stores. Unlike North America where everything is on sale all the time, Les Soldes somehow helps one put shopping into a perspective: other activities, such as eating, family and recreation take precedence over sales shopping.

∞

Like traditions in many countries, January is the time for new resolutions that often include exercise and activities. If you are staying in an area for more than a few weeks, you can get involved in a range of activities. Many towns and villages organize a wide variety of courses, exercise groups, excursions and historical activities. The local Mairie will be able to provide details regarding village contacts.

While France has a clear separation between Church and State, religious celebrations continue to play a strong part in the festival calendar. Christmas decorations invariably include a manger scene made up of numerous *Santons* (hand-carved figures.) Often, a community will organize a demonstration of these Santons. They are considered family treasures and handed down through generations. The carved figures are often very elaborate and feature, besides the traditional Christmas personalities, figures representing examples of Languedoc customs and trades. On a January walk in the countryside surrounding our village we ended up at a local Chateau and invited in to see their major, animated display of Santons and the Christmas scene.

∞

Much has been written about the food and markets of France-it's all true! Even in January, markets display a wide variety of local and seasonal produce, meats, cheeses, seafood and specialties of the region. January market days are surprisingly busy. They provide the motivation to come out from the wood fires and mingle with the neighbours.

Our fruit and vegetable lady, Bernadette, knows all her customers and how they like their produce. As she *taquines* (jests) with them, you understand the importance of these everyday village events. Now it is our turn-she carefully lifts out the various bits we have chosen and proceeds to describe how they should be prepared. The squash we have selected is a *courge violon* and she informs us that it is best prepared by first roasting it. As she lifts out the kiwi and the Belgian endive we have placed together in the green plastic bowl used to hold our selections, she patiently explains that it is not a good idea to mix the two as the hairs from the kiwi will infiltrate the endive and be ticklish to eat. She asks what we are using the vegetables for and I explain that I am making a veal stew. She realizes that I have not purchased any parsley-one cannot make a real veal stew without parsley and promptly adds a bunch to my order, saying *"un petit cadeau"* (a small gift).

Monique explains that the foods of January tend to focus on feasts and festivals and keeping warm and therefore, are laden with duck and goose fat, cheese and lots of calories. After all, winter is the time for laying on extra insulation to protect against the outdoor activities that still need to be done. Following are several recipes that are considered January staples. Monique has chosen three and we have adapted them to North American techniques. Enjoy.

GALETTE DU ROI

The first celebration aftcr New Year's is to mark Epiphany on January 6th. Monique explains that the symbol of this event is a cake that as she proud points out because her husband is from Brittany, is often served with apple cider. The north of France uses a cake called a "Galette du Roi" while in the south, the cake, that uses a brioche dough, is called a "Royaume". However, there doesn't seem to be a clear preference for either one and in fact, they are both delicious. All the stores were selling various sizes and shapes of the Galette du Roi to mark the upcoming feast of Epiphany. Monique's response when I mentioned that I wanted to buy one was "No, no, no, it is simple to make, we will make one together". So, here is Monique's recipe for Galette du Roi. If it is bought in a store, it always comes with a paper crown.

Ingredients:

Parchment paper large enough to hold the 12 inch pastry

Enough puff pastry to roll into two thin rounds of 12 inch diameter-use frozen store bought and follow thawing instructions.

Filling:

½ cup melted unsalted butter

¾ cup sugar

$^1/_2$ teaspoon vanilla

$^3/_4$ cup ground almonds

2 large eggs

Small china figurine for Galette du Roi cakes

1 egg, beaten for brushing on the crust

Optional-1 teaspoon rum or cognac

Preparation:

Remove middle oven rack and cover with a layer of parchment paper

Pre-heat oven to 350°F

Beat together the melted butter, sugar, vanilla, ground almonds (rum or cognac, if using) and eggs until smooth, thick batter-this is easy to do using a wooden spoon.

Lay first round of puff pastry directly on parchment paper on oven rack

Brush edge all around with beaten egg to provide stickiness to secure second layer

Pour almond mixture into the centre of the pastry. If you are adding a fève, place it in the almond mixture.

Place second pastry round on top and turn edges over to secure. Use fork to seal edges.

Make 1 inch hole in centre of top crust and roll a 2 inch piece of parchment paper into a cylinder shape to create a "chimney". Place into hole to allow excess heat to escape.

Score top with fork into three diagonal crisscross lines. Brush top of pastry with beaten egg.

Place oven rack in middle of 350°F oven. Check after 15 minutes-should be lightly golden-bake until golden brown, about another 10 minutes.

According to Monique, the French tradition and the proper way to serve this cake is to have the youngest member of the family sit under the table and call out who is to get the next piece. This prevents family squabbles from erupting over the fève. Once someone has found the fève in their piece of cake, they get to wear the crown and be king or queen for the day.

CHICKEN À LA MONIQUE

Monique made this for us for New Years and chicken never tasted so delicious. This recipe is for four persons but can be increased as needed, especially the sauce!

Ingredients for 4 people:

Chicken breast and thighs

¼ cup safflower or canola oil

½-1 teaspoon salt

Several grates fresh pepper

1 onion, chopped

1 tin sliced, white mushrooms, liquid discarded, or 1 cup sliced fresh mushrooms-may use morels but not other wild mushrooms

4 tablespoons crème fraiche, if not available, you can make your own by adding 2 tablespoons buttermilk to fresh cream and letting it sit for several hours.

½ cup Noilly Prat dry vermouth and ½ cup dry white wine or 1 cup dry white wine if Noilly Prat not available

Part 2: 2 tablespoons crème fraiche

1 egg yolk

Preparation:

In a large casserole, heat oil and add chicken pieces. Cook over medium heat until golden brown on all sides.

Add salt and pepper during cooking process

When browned, remove chicken to a plate and stir onions into remaining fat. Cook until lightly golden.

Add mushrooms to onions and simmer together for approximately 10 minutes, until onions are completely soft.

Remove mixture from heat and gently stir in 4 tablespoons crème fraiche until mixed completely

Return to low heat and simmer gently until mixture bubbles-approximately 5 minutes

Add in Noilly Prat and wine

Return chicken to pot and simmer together for another 15 minutes or until chicken is completely

cooked. Dish may be refrigerated at this time and re-heated later.

Re-heat approximately 30 minutes. Immediately before serving, mix together 2 tablespoons crème fraiche and beaten egg yolk until smooth. Mix small amounts of hot liquid into crème fraiche, egg yolk mixture to ensure that it doesn't curdle. Then add to meat mixture, stirring gently. Serve with salad, rice, lots of fresh baguette and a chilled, white Viognier or Rosé. This recipe also works well with veal.

ALIGOT

In all likelihood, every northern country has its own "rib-sticking" recipe for winter warmth, be it porridge, perogies or spaetzle. Languedoc has Aligot that comes specifically from the Lozere in the Haute Languedoc where villages and hamlets far outnumber towns and sheep and cows vastly outnumber people. It is a simple high protein, high fat dish made from local ingredients: potatoes, garlic and cheese.

In France, there are many varieties of potatoes, most of them not available in North America. In the markets or stores, there will be information as to the best use of each variety. The one most similar in cooking properties to Idaho potatoes would be the Bintje potatoes.

Ingredients for 4 people:

4-6 large boiling potatoes such as Yukon Gold

2 cups diced young Cantal or Tomme cheese
(mild Cheddar could be substituted)

1 cup crème fraiche

2 garlic cloves, mashed

Salt and pepper to taste

Preparation:

Boil potatoes, drain and mash, adding salt and pepper

Mix in cheese until mixture is creamy and stringy-best done by hand

Add crème fraiche and garlic and mix

This dish can be eaten all by itself but is a tasty accompaniment for homemade sausage and a *coustaud* (robust) red Minervois wine.

FEBRUARY

brocantes, winter sports, Limoux festival,
flower festivals, cooking classes

So much for the warm temperatures of January-while
most days are still sunny, February can be cold and rarely there
may be a light snowfall. However, as one friend said "by the time
I find my camera, it's melted." It's not uncommon in February
for the freezing winds from Siberia to rush down through
central France bringing with them plunging temperatures of
3-4°C with -5° at night (37°F). Warm underwear, heavy coats
and good heating systems are *de rigeur* (required) in February, at
least for a short time. However, with Languedoc in sunshine for

300 days of the year, even these cold days offer rays of warmth if one can find a secluded, protected area.

> Within two weeks of struggling with long under-wear, puffy coats, scarves, and coats, we were exchanging them for light jackets, swimsuits and sunglasses. Spring had arrived and with it 20°C temperatures, almond blossoms, longer days and sunbathing at the beach. The street noises started as we all opened our windows to chase out the winter air and let in the warm sunshine of late February.

All this means is that February in Languedoc is great for people who like to ski, aren't put off by dramatic temperature changes, want to check out *brocantes* (antique shops) and *vide greniers* (garage sales) before the rush, love landscape painting and want to become more involved in French communities.

∞

> As we ventured out into the cold, others met us in their puffy down jackets, boots and fur hats. Neighbours still greeted us with "Bonjour Monsieursdames" however, for those who know us, they delighted in teasing us about how we must be used to this cold as we came from Canada. This was invariably followed by a typical French gesture to signify either extreme cold or hot. To practice the gesture, hold your fingers closely together and with your hand held

rigid, shake it rapidly for 3-4 shakes holding it closely to your face-almost as though you were drying your nail polish. For a truly French effect while doing the gesture, say "O-la-la."

∞

The cold doesn't stop people from going out and participating in the month's festivals. February festivals include the February feast of St Blaise, the patron saint of the nearby town of Pezanas and the harbinger of spring. Many of the festivals are rooted in pagan rituals and celebrate abundance and fertility. The local parade features huge papier marché bulls sporting gigantic testicles around which are wrapped grape leaves-both powerful symbols in Languedoc.

Over a two-day period in February, Pezanas celebrated the Festival of St Blaise, a beloved bishop in medieval times. The first day was a major celebration with a parade down the main boulevard of the town. A local resident dressed as St Blaise left the church, mounted a donkey backwards as the ritual indicated and proceeded to parade throughout the main streets of the centre ville. It is believed that his blessings bring on an early spring and auspicious planting opportunities. Along with the bishop, came the animal symbols of the outlying villages. These village mascots, for example our village has a cerf, a deer like animal, that is possibly an ancient name for the village, are called totemiques. They have huge molded heads, some with horns or antlers, they are made of decorated fabric, stand about eight feet tall, may have anatomical aberrations such as huge testicles and are paraded around by 8-10 male villagers chosen for their strength who stand underneath to carry the "animal". We watched in amazement as several totemiques engaged in mock battles with each other displaying the ability and agility of the team to maneuver the animal plus keep the head engaged in the battle. There was great glee from the people lining the streets as their animals jostled each other. The enthusiasm and hilarity of the audience helped ward off the cold but as the parade passed by, the crowds quickly faded into the bars lining the street. Not to forget the ecclesiastical element, the following day was a church celebration but few people attended that!

∞

In the town of Limoux, one of the oldest, continuous festivals in Europe happens from mid-January to Easter. In the middle ages, so the story goes, the millers of the town began this celebration to mark their successful trading with the kingdom of Aragon. The Fécos, an Occitan dance, happens three times a day on Saturday and Sunday in the central arcaded square. The dance steps are the same but each dance troupe is made up of a different team from either the town or a neighbouring locale.

The costumes have evolved over the centuries and some now resemble Carnival costumes from Venice.

After visiting Cathar sites in Queribus and Rennes le Chateau, we continued along and wandered into Limoux on a cool February afternoon around 4PM. Limoux is known for a large, central arcade and wonderful cafés so we headed there only to be confronted with a mass of revelers and unusual drumming and horn sounds. Following the crowds, we came across an extraordinary sight. Moving slowly under the arcade was a dancing troupe of beautifully dressed and masked phenomenally tall people. On closer inspection, we realized that they were wearing high boots concealed under their dresses. While the costumes were spectacular, it was the mesmerizing movements of their dance, the Fécos, that caught our attention. The rhythm was slow, repetitive but wonderfully haunting. They chanted in words that we could not understand but that someone said was Occitan, the ancient dialect of Languedoc. The dancers proceeded around the entire arcade, taking over an hour to slowly navigate the area. One of the highlights of the event was that at certain points in the dance, they would toss out candies, oranges or other small treats to the crowds. The children would scatter among the dancers trying to grab the objects flying through the air. The magic for us was being part of an event that traced its roots back to medieval times. Like much of life here in Languedoc, the festivals, celebrations and customs are part of the *patrimonie*, the rootedness of the culture.

∞

Languedoc has primarily a Mediterranean climate with some regional variations in the high Languedoc, such as up on the limestone *causses* (barren, windswept mountains). This means that even in February, palm, mimosa, citrus and olive trees flourish in the warm sun beaming down on hidden valleys. One particular place enjoys a microclimate that allows for early blossoming and its own festival. Roquebrun is nestled in the foothills of the Montagne Noire, protected from the Siberian winds and the hills warmed by the south facing exposure. In late February, with the mimosa is full bloom, well ahead of other regions of Languedoc, the town hosts the first of several annual regional flower festivals.

Sundays are different from the work week in France as it is often the only day off for many people; children typically have classes on Saturday morning, stores and many offices are open as usual, and with the work day running until 7:30PM, there isn't time for after work activities. Therefore, cultural events are typically planned for Sunday.

The Midi Libre, the regional newspaper, alerted us to two Sunday events that caught our eye: the Abbaye de Cassan was holding one of its monthly Sunday morning concerts and the Mimosa Festival was on in Roquebrun. We could, with a bit of planning, take in both events and still have a leisurely lunch somewhere. After breakfast, off we went to the eleventh century Chateau de Cassan that has been recently updated and is now open to the public. The concert featured a violist and a pianist and was held in one of the reception room. The tapistried walls, tall windows overlooking the vineyard and the elegant, hand-decorated grand piano made us feel slightly underdressed in our jeans and jackets. Surely, a silk gown and powdered wig would have been a more appropriate ensemble. However, we realized from the conversations around us that the reason people were here was the music. The two musicians treated us to a lovely concert of music by French composers. The morning closed with a wine tasting from a local vigneron and a chance to chat with friends. After leaving the reception, we headed to the mimosa festival in Roquebrun.

We approached this medieval town from the southeast, passing along the rising hills that surround the town. The hillside was covered in the yellow flowering trees of the mimosa. Further along, as we turned into Roquebrun we could see the houses rising steeply up the side of the hill, each row higher than the other with the church tower holding court over all. The town flows down from the hillside to the river Orb in the valley below with barely enough flat land to provide for the one main street that traverses the town. Parking would be a nightmare, even for a day in February. However, the planners were ready for the hoards and parking was available down on the flats by the river. The Orb is wide at this point and filled with great flat rocks that allow transit to the other side-at least if the water level is low enough. By now, we were hungry and found a wonderful restaurant perched out over the river below, providing a panoramic view of the valley. As is so typical of February menus in Languedoc, the food was hearty, flavourful and we did not need a bank loan for our four courses. The appetizer of creamy soup, main course of duck breast and trimmings, cheese plate and dessert cost 20E and that included a glass of wine, coffee, taxes and tip.

Roquebrun, because of its topography, can only be accessed by foot. Fortunately, we had eaten well and could now burn those calories. In addition to the mimosa displays, there was an afternoon parade, numerous tables set up for wine tastings and an open buffet for sampling local foods. We spent the afternoon wandering and sampling-food, wine, colour and beauty. By 5:30 we made our way back home but one last surprise awaited us. Parked at the exit to a major roundabout, sat the local *Gendarmes* (Police) carrying out breathalyzer tests on drivers. There is a concerted effort being made throughout France to reduce drunk driving and knowing what Sundays are like, it is a key day for catching the unwary driver. Fortunately, we were fine and made it home safely. There is a law being passed in France that requires all vehicles to have two breathalyzer kits at all times. If the driver has been drinking, he or she is supposed to use one kit before they start driving. The other kit is used if the driver is stopped by the police. The practice of demanding to see the kits is not widespread throughout France but it is better to be safe than sorry. The fines for impaired driving are very steep and foreign drivers are not exempted from the penalties. There is no penalty for using a non-French driving license.

∞

There is one day in February that is celebrated in France quite differently from the North America version and that is the feast of St. Valentin. North American customs typically center on cards, flowers and chocolate for everyone. In France, it is a much bigger celebration and focuses much more on partners and couples. Fine restaurants offer lavish multi course meals for the amorous couple; gold jewelry seems to be a required gift and chocolate confections are more elaborate in each passing shop window. It makes sense that in the country where people sing so well of "l'amour", the feast of St Valentin would be a major celebration.

∞

Cold, windy days in February offer a perfect excuse for brocanting and there is no better place than Languedoc for French antiques. Pezenas and surrounding towns have become well known centers for the antique market and many of the main stores will ship items internationally. There are also weekend bricabrac fairs in several surrounding communities. By February, the first of the *vide-greniers* (garage sale) will start and they offer bargains not likely to be found in your hometown. Depending on what your interest is, Pezenas offers something for all antique lovers-old lace and linen, massive old furniture and small items that make interesting souvenirs.

> The temperature was going down to 6°C today and we wanted to have a chance to explore Pezenas but keep out of the cold winds. This was our chance to check out the antique shops. The window gave little idea of what was inside except the small, handwritten wooden sign "Linges Anciens", led us to expect that we would find old lace and linens. On entering the store, it was hard to tell if it was closed or not until a voice from the back called out "Bonjour Mesdames, entrées." All the merchandise looked quite jumbled compared to the orderliness we expect from stores at home. However, it was soon clear that everything

had a place and it was easy to navigate the tables of wares. Linen bedsheets, counterpanes and pillowcases covered several tables. At first, I wasn't sure about the prices as I had checked out similar items at home. Was it possible that these linen sheets were only 20 Euros (1 euro = approx. 75 cents) each? "Yes, that was correct", said madame, sitting perched on her stool. Lying on one table, looking quite out of place, was a burnished tan leather handbag that caught my eye. While I did not need another handbag, it certainly was beautiful and clearly vintage. It had just arrived and madame had not even put it up for sale. Somehow, it called out to me and madam and I negotiated a price. As she was wrapping it, she mentioned that it was a style used by women in the French resistance during the Second World War. It seemed somewhat providential that the next evening there was a documentary on TV about women in the French resistance and I'm sure that I saw the same handbag. I continually receive comments from people of all ages about it and where it came from. This one random purchase has provided me with endless opportunities to share stories with various people about life here in Languedoc—priceless!

The bricabrac sales offer the chance to purchase items that would likely never be seen back home—the antique can which hangs near our front door, the sterling silver olive picker-uppers we found for 3 Euros, the fine lace and linen hankies and the armoires that take the place of cupboards because old houses do not have built-ins. I almost missed the small ad for the local vide-grenier but off we went on Sunday morning to a neighbouring village. Obviously, I wasn't the only one who saw the ad; the grounds were packed—this was your community garage sale! The items being offered ranged from those that would have you asking "why would you bother" to those over which you would exclaim "do you have any idea what this is worth". Armed with our "must have" list, we picked through a number of tables as we practised good bargaining and acting skills—how badly do I want this item and is my enthusiasm showing too much? In the end, we spent about 10E and came away with more mismatched dishes to add to our growing collection. Even for a casual visitor, it's a chance to participate in a multicultural experience, spend a Sunday morning in the warm sunshine and perhaps, come away with a few treasures, providing you're willing to check out the merchandise and engage with the sellers.

∞

Unlike school systems in North America, children in the French school system are exposed to a more rigorous education in problem solving and debate. This is evident in the array of exercise books for children of all ages, grades and subjects that are on display in bookstores and supermarkets. In addition to schoolwork and homework, children are encouraged to continue their studies during holidays and weekends by completing the workbooks that are designed to follow the national school curriculum.

Not only children but adults are encouraged to maintain skills in certain areas such as critical thinking and debate. This is evident in the television programming, the newspapers and literature and the wide range of accredited courses available even in small villages. There is considerable emphasis on exploring points of view, understanding other perspectives and finding compromise. One opportunity for a visitor to Languedoc, especially in February when it's good to be inside on a windy afternoon, is to participate in a *café philosophe*, (discussion club).

> The new couple we met shared with us their experience of attending a café philo that encouraged communication between English and French speakers. What a great idea and so off we went to the café philo in the neighbouring town. The gathering was held in the smallest restaurant we had ever seen-20 seats maximum and all the tables were squeezed closely together. On our visit, however, there were only five people-three English-speaking (although one was from England and had such a broad accent, we could not understand most of what he said in English) and two French-speakers. Madame, the owner,

hosted the event and opened the discussion. This time, as we were new, it was more a "getting to know you" afternoon. She offered coffee and wine choices and at the end of ninety minutes of pleasant conversation, it was time to go. Her response when we went to pay was "Non, un petit cadeau." This gesture, that we have encountered so often, has led us to appreciate that people in Languedoc understand that there are more important elements than money: courtesy, kindness, friendship, and engagement.

∞

The demographics in France are similar to most of North America in that the baby boomers are taking over. This is equally true in Languedoc although it is nothing like Florida or Arizona with their retirement villages. In Languedoc, it means that many towns and villages are developing a wide range of interests to engage the retired members of their communities, many of whom are moving here from other parts of France or other countries. These activities allow visitors to become involved in more traditional, non-tourist pursuits in the off-season. In February, visitors can join in a variety of events, such as a series of classes on the region's history, cooking, art, chess or pottery. For someone staying longer than a month, it may mean a joining fee to participate but for single events, the price is reasonable for an event that often features food and wine along at the end of the class.

We had met Josianne on one of the local walks and she encouraged us to attend the upcoming *soupe et contes* (soup & stories) evening being hosted by the local Art et Culture committee. We had seen the sign posted at the Tabac for the event but were not sure who could attend. "Absolument," she said, when we asked if it was open to visitors. The storyteller had already begun when we arrived and I was astonished to hear her recount *Le Soupe de Cailloux* (Stone Soup), a story I had told my own children so often. She was followed by a man who used song and rhyme to recount stories of life in Languedoc. Those gathered around clearly knew the words and were soon singing along to his melody. Our participation was greatly enhanced by the bottles of wine on the table and the frequent pouring by the gentleman sitting across from me. The story hour was followed by a soup buffet that the women of the committee had prepared for us. The bowls were "bottomless" and with a little encouragement from others at the table, we sampled potato and leek, creamy chestnut, squash and bacon, broccoli and pureed vegetable soups. Over the course of the meal, we chatted with another couple who had moved to our village from Paris and were also enjoying retirement in Languedoc. We compared notes in our halting French and English and we all agreed that these evenings were a wonderful way to meet new friends and neighbours regardless of how far we had come. We ended the evening by arranging to meet them for drinks. This is how friendships begin in Languedoc-over wine, food and large tables.

∞

Languedoc offers two regions-the Pyrenees in western Languedoc and the Cevennes in the Haute Languedoc both featuring family-oriented ski opportunities. The Pyrenees offers first class resorts such as Font Romeu and Les Angles. Monique says that the sunshine, hot springs, fine powder and smaller crowds combine to provide a better experience than the Alps. The Cevenne resorts offer miles of spectacular cross-country trails and limited short ski runs. Prat Peyrot and Mas de la Barque both feature great trails. Compared to the Alps, skiing in Languedoc is much cheaper yet resorts are able to meet the needs of beginner to advanced skiers.

> We couldn't figure out why there were suddenly no children in the street and the market days looked so different. Monique indicated that it was "les vacances du ski"- the winter holiday devoted to outdoor winter activities. For families who were not visiting the local ski hills, it became apparent that *mami et papi* (grandma & grandpa) were doing child care as suddenly older adults were at the market with small children in tow.

While there is excellent childcare readily available at reasonable cost for children as young as two years of age, many families in Languedoc still live with extended families nearby and grandparents and aunties are often main caregivers for both children and elderly parents.

∞

It has been said that the winter light of Languedoc inspires artists with its clarity and the way colours come alive. From the Cote Vermeille of Collioure to Arles, Languedoc offers inspiration around every corner.

> I drove over the hill and before me, set against the afternoon winter sky were the green tiled turrets of the chateau hovering over the approaching hamlet. The golden sandstone of the towers outlined against the azure blue of the sky made me stop the car in awe of the beauty. Later, I spoke to my art teacher about the light and his comment was that the February sun filters the light in a purer way and gives colours a trueness that is not present at other times of the year. He explained this was because the Sirocco winds from the Sahara no longer fill the air with sand, bending the light rays and distorting our vision. Suddenly, we began to see the landscapes around us differently, to appreciate the crispness of the scenes and the richness of the colours. Our camera became a necessary tool as we ventured out. By the end of February, as the days warmed and the wind picked up, the scenes began to lose some of their clarity and brightness. It made

us realize that this was yet another of the small pleasures of life in February in Languedoc.

For those interested in painting and photography, February offers the opportunity to access courses or private lessons. A photographer friend in a neighbouring village has set up tutoring classes for the advanced photographer. Most villages of any size offer an array of art classes. This month is an excellent time to discover or expand talents.

∞

We have rarely participated in a conversation in France without somehow wandering to the topic of food. Even on discussions that start out being erudite and dry, somehow, ultimately, food becomes the topic of the conversation. This food focus is translating into courses and classes in smaller towns all across Languedoc and is aimed primarily at visitors or people settling here from another country.

> We were almost finished the dinner meal at the B&B and were about to begin the fruit course at the end. The cherries looked wonderful but my table mate could not eat them so I offered to finish hers. As I reached for my water glass, Matilde, the hostess, leapt across the table to me and stopped me from reaching for my water glass-"non, non, non, ni melons, ni cerises", all the time wagging her finger in that quintessential French way. She went on to explain that water interferes with the acidity of melons and

cherries and should not be taken together. This was the first of many lessons in food combining and preparation that were always given with our best interests at heart and with the firm belief in their validity.

For a real experience in French cooking, there are numerous possibilities throughout Languedoc to take a class from a local chef or arrange a private wine tasting tour. The best places to check for these courses are the local newspaper, Midi Libre, the Herault and Aude Times, Crème de Languedoc and The BBB Midi. All of them have good websites.

> We had arranged for the four of us to take a cooking class with David, a young chef in the village who offers classes in French cuisine. We arrived at his kitchen where he explained that we would be working around the piano. He laughed when he realized how perplexed we looked. He explained that in French cooking there are many musical terms-a *mandoline*, is an instrument used for slicing, a *violon* is a type of squash, a *chef* can also refer to a choral conductor and *piano* refers to a stovetop.

> The four-hour class consisted of each of us assisting in preparing a multiple-course lunch under his guidance and then joining together in the dining room to eat our results. His patience and careful instructions enabled us to sit down at noon to individual vegetable terrine starters,

poached salmon in a papiotte crust and pepper colis, tied asparagus, citron mousse and chocolate fondant. This was accompanied by local wines, liquors and coffee. Afterwards, we ambled down the hill to home in good form bathed in the mid-afternoon sun.

∞

On telephone posts all over the region, there are notices of *Lotos*-these are fundraising get-togethers over food and drink. The main purpose is to sell raffle tickets for a wide variety of prizes. The events are organized by all sorts of groups from the *Sapeurs-Pompiers* (firefighters) to schools, art and rugby clubs. Prizes range from bottles of local wine, honey or produce to tickets or items from local merchants. More importantly, they offer a chance to mingle in a fun, easy milieu with your neighbours.

> The posters all around the village announcing the upcoming Loto promised an evening of fun and great prizes to be won. Off we went to see what was going on. The *Salle des Fetes* (community hall) was packed and the adults were laughing and catching up on the local gossip while the children ran around greeting friends. It was Friday night and people were glad for the end of the work week. We all headed to the drinks table for glasses of wine and then found spots at long tables for the evening's event.

Monique has mentioned that these are popular gatherings as they are a great way for people to get together as very little entertaining is done in peoples' homes. Sure enough, we met neighbours and made new friends as we chatted throughout the evening. We were however, a bit surprised when we issued an invitation to come for dinner. The response seemed cool and finally, the couple indicated that this would not be possible. Unsure of what we had done wrong, we asked a friend who explained that in French culture, there are many small steps to be taken in developing a friendship before one is invited to share a meal in a person's home. In fact, it could be years before the relationship is deemed strong enough to permit such an invitation. She explained that homes and sharing meals are for family therefore, one must earn the right to be considered family. Understanding these cultural differences makes our encounters more meaningful and richer. It was a special honour for us when Monique and Pierre first invited us to dinner.

∞

Like many activities, hunting in France is considered a *droit* (a right) and is governed by strict laws. For example, winter hunting is restricted to Saturday and Sunday mornings in January and February. The main target for hunters in winter is the *sanglier*, the wild boar that has now overrun the south of

France and are a nuisance to farmers and grape growers. When out walking in the fields, small roads and byways, one does need to be careful about wandering among the vineyards and fields on Saturday and Sunday mornings. Unfortunately, every year in France some unsuspecting walker gets mistaken for a sanglier or deer. Not a pleasant memory of a trip to Languedoc.

Monique and I were out driving around the back roads in our area when I commented on the men appearing to survey in the field beside us. There were two men with tripods set up and waiting patiently. Monique explained that they were hunters and there would be others in the field on our other side who would be using dogs to chase the wild boar towards the hunters giving them a good chance to shoot the animal. So, here we were caught between the two groups awaiting the arrival of the sanglier. We wasted no time in moving out of there.

∞

February in Languedoc means hearty fare to warm you up, store some fat and prepare you to withstand the mistral and Tramontane winds that whistle down from northern Europe and are funneled down to Languedoc through the Montagne Noire and the Pyrenees. Monique chose three well known Languedocienne recipes that feature prominently this month: cassoulet, tartiflette, chicken marengo and crepes. Each of these dishes comes with its own history lesson.

CASSOULET

As Monique describes it, "cassoulet is more than a main course, it is a legend". In the middle ages, so the story goes, the town of Castelnaudry was besieged by invaders. The townspeople were down to their last food supplies and would have to surrender or else starve to death. The chiefs called the people together to prepare a communal dish that would give them the strength to repel the enemy. The result is that there is a mythology to this dish and it is seen as an emblem of Languedoc and its history of courage and resilience in hard times.

The official recipe dictates that a true cassoulet must be made with white beans and water from the Lauraugais, the area and river immediately surrounding Castlenaudry. The water is particularly hard and allows the beans to retain their shape over the hours of cooking. It is said that the best cassoulet comes from the farmers wives and it is considered a true peasant fare.

Monique reminded me that the secret to a delicious cassoulet is the *seven skins*. This refers to the long slow cooking time and the need to pierce the top of the cassoulet seven times over the cooking period to allow air to escape. Like most French recipes, one can argue for hours as to what constitutes *un vrai cassoulet (an authentic dish)*. Consensus indicates that in addition to white beans and water, garlic, onions, carrots, duck, sausage and herbs are typical ingredients. This is a dish to be savoured with a robust red wine from the region, baguettes and good friends. Be sure to allow several hours and loose belts for this meal.

Ingredients for 8 persons:

2 pounds dry white beans

½ cup duck fat

½ cup fresh pork rind

½ pound chopped bacon

1 ½ pounds pork shoulder, cubed

2 duck legs and thighs, in pieces

1 small garlic sausage

1 cup sausages, Toulouse or other mild sausage

1 cup chopped onion

4 garlic cloves

2 bouquet garni-springs of thyme, rosemary, bay leaves and oregano tied together with string

6 tomatoes, pulp only

1 carrot

1 onion picked with 3 whole cloves

1-2 cups breadcrumbs

Salt & pepper

Andrea Swan with Monique Guezel

Preparation:

Now the ritual: soak the beans for at least 3 hours in cold water. Then, rinse in clean water.

Place beans in large Dutch oven, add ¼ cup duck fat, pork rind, bouquet garni, carrot, two cloves of garlic and onion with cloves. Cover mixture with water and place over medium heat on stovetop.

When the mixture comes to a boil, salt lightly, make sure it remains covered with water and lower the heat until it continues to boil gently. Continuing cooking until the beans begin to soften. This can take up to 4 hours of boiling time.

When the beans have cooked for about 2 hours, you can start to prepare the remainder of the ingredients. After seasoning the meats with salt and pepper, brown the duck pieces and the pork cubes in duck fat. Then add the diced onions, remaining garlic cloves and bouquet garni. Cover and let simmer, adding a bit of the bean liquid to keep the meat moist.

Brown the sausages separately and set aside, having poured off the excess fat.

When the beans are almost cooked, add the tomato pulp, the meat mixture, the garlic and Toulouse sausages that have been cut into 1-2 inch pieces.

Now you are at the crucial part: in a deep-sided casserole dish, layer the ingredients, starting with the bean mixture, followed by the meats. Remember to give a grind of pepper on each layer.

Once all the ingredients have been layered into the dish, you put the finishing touch on by covering the top with the fine breadcrumbs.

Then, with great ceremony, you place the dish in the oven and leave it, as Monique says, "for a long incubation period". This means several hours in a low oven at 250-300°F.

To follow the tradition exactly means to perform the ritual of the "seven skins". Pierce the crust seven times over the slow baking period. Serve with plenty of bread, a simple green salad and a hearty red Cotes de Rhone wine. In Monique's opinion, the sign of a successful cassoulet is the "religious silence" of tasting the first bit of cassoulet. Enjoy!

TARTIFLETTE

Tartiflette is another regional specialty that draws on simple, plentiful food. The recipe in this case, like aligot, includes potatoes and cheese. However, as in French cooking, the ingredients used should not be interchanged-otherwise, the recipe is considered incorrect and may warrant a shaking of the finger.

Monique explained that, unlike other traditional French dishes, tartiflette is a relative newcomer. In the 1980s, in response to dropping sales, the Roblechon cheesemakers created this dish as a way to expand their market. They certainly did a terrific job as this is a Languedoc favourite and found in many local cookbooks. However, as Monique pointed out, each village and often individual cooks, will be adamant that their recipe is the *vrai* tartiflette. Tartiflette is made with Robluchon cheese and contains *lardons.* Bacon, as it is sold in North America, is hard to find in France. The closest substitute is the cubed lardons that are a staple in several winter recipes. Monique describes this dish as *bouratif (*rib sticking*)*. It is best served with only a green salad, baguette and a glass of red St. Chinian wine if you want to be able to get up from the table. It is probably best to make this for the dinner meal, as there is a tendency to want to snuggle up with a warm blanket in front of a blazing fire after this meal.

Ingredients for 4 persons:

3 pounds potatoes such as Yukon Gold

1 cup of lardons or cubed thick, sliced bacon

1 cup finely chopped onion

1 round of Robluchon cheese, this can now be found in many specialty cheese counters across North America.

1 cup dry white wine

Salt and pepper to taste

Preparation:

Boil peeled potatoes in salted water until they can be pieced easily with a sharp knife.

When ready, rinse and slice potatoes in thick rounds

Lightly butter an oval, ovenproof serving dish

Layer together the onions, potatoes and lardons

Drizzle wine over mixture

Salt and pepper liberally

Cut Roblochon into half and place both half rounds horizontally on top of mixture

Bake in 350-400°F oven until Roblochon is melted and golden on top-about 20-30minutes

CHICKEN MARENGO

Although this may sound like a Spanish dish, it is quite at home in Languedoc. Monique insists that the secret to this dish is to use whole chicken, not just chicken breasts.

Ingredients for 6 persons:

1 chicken (4 lbs) cut into pieces

4 tomatoes, cubed, if in season, otherwise, 1
14 ounce can of whole or cubed tomatoes

2 medium onions coarsely diced

3 cloves minced garlic

1 cup small, button mushrooms

1 cup white wine

4 tablespoons olive oil

2 tablespoons butter

1 bay leave

1 teaspoon dried thyme-2 teaspoons if using fresh

$^1\!/_4$ cup chopped parsley-to garnish

Salt & pepper to taste

Preparation:

In a large pan, sauté the chicken pieces in the olive oil until golden. Remove and set aside

Add the onions and sauté until golden

Then add all the remaining ingredients except the parsley, and let simmer for about 50 minutes.

Just before serving, transfer to heated casserole dish and garnish with parsley.

Serve with rice or broad noodles. A white Picpoul de Pinet is a good wine accompaniment.

CREPES

The evening meal of Mardi Gras in France is similar to what North Americans call Pancake Tuesday. It represents the cleaning out of the fat, eggs and rich foods in preparation for the Lenten season. In previous societies, it represented the last of plentiful food as people entered the lean months before the arrival of the first foods of spring. In France, there are two types of crepes-savoury and sweet. The savoury crepes are called *galettes* and made with buckwheat flour so are a good alternative for anyone who is gluten intolerant. They are filled with an extraordinary range of savory foods such as eggs, spinach, seafood, bacon, ham, cured meats, and typically reflect regional specialties both in ingredients and in name.

Sweet crepes are made with white flour and again the fillings defy the imagination with their possibilities but will typically include whipping cream, caramel, liqueurs, fruits and nuts.

In the town of Pezenas, there is a small restaurant, La Cour Pavée that features the galettes and crepes of Brittany. They have one memorable crepe called Le Menhir, named after the large, single, standing monoliths found throughout northern Europe. Le Menhir is filled with homemade salted caramel and is melt-in-your-mouth delicious. This is one dish that is difficult to share!

If you want to enjoy crepes and galettes on your own, the local supermarkets in France sell pre-made crepes and then it is up to your imagination to discover what taste treats emerge.

MARCH

Roman roads, terrace meals & fresh food,
book lovers, Cathars, spring foods

March in Languedoc is for those who want to wander the countryside, feeling the warm sun on their faces, see yellow erupt everywhere with the blossoming of the mimosa, gorse and forsythia, explore Roman ruins, haunt centuries old book stores, and feast on the first foods of spring.

While the museums of Agde and Narbonne provide wonderful examples of artifacts from the area, there is nothing that compares to walking Roman roads that are still used by locals to connect communities and provide quiet shortcuts between villages.

The map indicated that this would be the Via Domitia, part of the Roman road joining Spain to Italy. We set off on a bright Sunday morning in early March. The path was marked with a small stone carving showing a drawing of a Roman chariot; it was about one small car width wide and a combination of cobblestones and broken pavement. What was interesting about it was the straightness of the road and the height above the surrounding fields. At one point, the road had fallen away and we could see the layers of roadbed built centuries ago. We were standing on a 2000 year old road that still today serves the local inhabitants! As we stood and marveled at this, an elderly gentleman wheeled his old, coaster bicycle up the incline and proceeded to explain how this road connected various villages in several directions. At least, we think that's what he said. His lack of teeth and the thick languedocienne accent made conversation rather difficult. What was in no doubt, however, was his willingness to stop and engage with two naïve Canadians and share his knowledge of the area.

The path led us to the remains of a Roman palace on the outskirts of Lespignan. In an attempt to raise the profile of Roman occupation all along the coast, the government has supported the excavation and restoration of numerous sites. The sites tend to be simply signposted without elaborate attempts to highlight the remains. These are simply part of the ongoing story of life in Languedoc.

∞

Vacation time for many people is a time to get caught up on one's reading. March in Languedoc offers plenty of opportunity for that, especially if one also enjoys rummaging through vintage, second hand bookstores for hidden treasures and antique bindings. A recent article in the *BBBMidi* magazine explained how France has three "book towns", villages that have a long-established reputation for their bookstores, are centers of bookbinding or are home to a literary community. One of these centers is in the heart of Languedoc in the small town on Montolieu. With a population of less than 1000 inhabitants, it has fifteen bookshops, a Centre des Arts & Métiers where one can take courses in all aspects of book making and paper arts and the remains of a Royal Manufacturing centre, set up during the reign of Louis XIV in 1740 to produce the Royal papers and books. The Royal Manufacturing buildings have now been turned into a plush vacation spa.

> We set out in the early afternoon and took the D11 road that runs through numerous small towns and close by the Canal du Midi on our way to Montolieu. Even though Languedoc covers approximately 16,500 sq. miles, an area the size of the Netherlands, it offers diverse geographical

and architectural variations. As we left behind the terra cotta roofs and sandstone houses of the southern Languedoc, the buildings transitioned to grey limestone rock walls with black slate tile roofs. These changes in architecture paralleled the changing landscape as we moved from the lowlands of the river valleys to the ravines of the Montagne Noire. The terrain around Montolieu rises up quickly from the Carcassonne basin of the river Aude and the town itself sits perches atop the highest local peak. The rapids of nearby river La Dure fuelled the turbines of the eighteenth century mills. The streets were narrow and winding and restricted to local vehicles. On this Sunday afternoon, we found many bookshops opened and booksellers happy to share their knowledge and treasures with us. Michael had come from the Netherlands 30 years ago for a holiday and like numerous others, had found his home in Montolieu. He had taken over the bookshop several years ago after the owner had died and he explained to us how the town had acquired a reputation and official recognition. Although I didn't find the titles I was looking for, the scent and feel of this old building was an unexpected treasure in itself. Michael encouraged us to visit other bookstores in the town that might have what I was searching for. Alas, I did not come away with any books but did spend a lovely warm, sunny afternoon wandering from one old book haunt to another, browsing among titles that I added to my "must read" list.

Leaving Montolieu behind, we travelled to another small book centre on the other side of Carcassonne. In the tiny village of Le Somail, along the banks of the Canal du Midi sits a bookstore that is reputed to be one of the oldest in France. With over 50,000 titles, we lost ourselves to the pleasure of browsing through myriad titles and corners. After making our selections, we sat on the bank of the canal with our coffee and croissants. Does it get better than this on a sunny March afternoon?

∞

If seeing more of the opulence of Louis XIV interests you, then a visit to Villeneuvette is in order. Unlike Montolieu with its village surrounding the Royal Manufacturing buildings, Villeneuvette, near Clermont L'Herault, is a free standing, walled town originally dedicated to the manufacture of linens and material for soldiers' uniforms. It housed the workers and was completely self-contained. Built in 1677, the town ceased manufacturing cloth only in 1955. The mills no longer operate and the homes are now privately owned. However, it is open to the public and the walks leading out from the town offer a wonderful view of the surrounding hills heading up to the Haute Languedoc.

It is easy to organize an outdoor day when the weather is warm and the sun is shining down. We started out with a walk through Villeneuvette, admiring the carefully laid streets and remarked how it resembled some northern French town characteristic of the Louis XIV architectural style. It was so unlike much of Languedoc style of the same period. We marveled at the far-reaching effects of the Sun King to make his artistic mark on his realm. At the edge of the village, we found the marked trail leading up into the hills and encountered an elderly lady and her companion returning from their walk. Her only walking aid was her cane as she ambled toward us. We were encouraged that if she could do it, then the sign indicating an easy trail would be accurate. For the most part, it was- a firm, hard packed, easy to walk trail with clearly identified markers to point the way forward. However, I did not consider the climb up the loose stones of the dry streambed to be part of an easy trail. But with walking and hiking so embedded in French culture, one can understand that it is a question of relative experience and expectations. We carried on and were well rewarded at the top with the view of the countryside.

From Villeneuvette, it is only 22 miles (30kms) to Herepian and the start of the Passa Pais voie verte, the recently reconstructed walking and cycling trail along the old rail line between Bedarieux and Mazemet. Again, we set out on the now bright, warm, late Sunday afternoon and continued our exploration of the past. Arriving in Lamalou les Bains, we settled into the first bar and watched as people walked slowly by, many of them with crutches or other mobility devices. For Lamalou les Bains, with its hot and cold thermal mineral springs, is an historical centre for curing a variety of diseases. In France, there is still a strong belief in the curative power of a range of alternative medical practices. In fact, a physician is just as likely to order *le cure* as a medication for a wide variety of ailments. As we walked around, it was obvious that Lamalou has passed the heyday although there are efforts being made to renew and update its reputation as a health rehabilitation destination. It was late afternoon when we headed back to Herepian and by now, the Sunday afternoon walkers were out in full force. The quiet months in Languedoc provide for these wonderfully French experiences. Profitez-bien.

∞

The south of France has a remarkably different climate from the north. With its mild winters and hot summers, it truly is a Mediterranean climate much like Greece, Spain, Italy and North Africa. As such, rain is an important element and arrives with great anticipation, usually during late October and late March. The rains are heavy, short lived and can quickly change the landscape dramatically. There is a good reason for some of the odder building techniques seen in the towns and country-side. In the old centre villes, all streets slope into the centre to allow rainwater to flow down to the rivers and streams. Most villages have floodways to divert the rapidly rising streams of the "rainy" season away from basements and subterranean caves.

> Spring came late this March as the rains seemed to persist for much longer than usual. Monique explained that *les giboulées de mars* (sleet storms) are the early sign that spring rains are coming. Depending on the severity of the these fierce, short-lived storms that hail down on the region, they act as predictors of the amount of rain coming to fill up the reservoirs and water tables and are harbingers of a good harvest in late summer. During the late afternoon sunshine when the four women gathered on the low stone wall to capture the few rays of the past week, they reminisced about various giboulées of the past fifty years and the effects of too much or too little rain in March.

∞

Beginning in the eleventh century, Languedoc was home to the Cathar sect. This offshoot of Catholicism developed quietly over several decades and flourished from east of Beziers to Toulouse amid the stable and relatively well-educated populace of the region. The end came for them because of the wealth they held, their threat to established papal rule with their alternative beliefs about the role, power and behaviour of the clergy and the desire by the French king to consolidate Languedoc under his rule. Unlike the crusades to the middle east, this twenty-year crusade mounted by the Pope and the King of France was the only crusade against a local population. Many of the horrific techniques practiced by the armies and Catholic monks during this crusade became hallmarks of the subsequent Spanish Inquisition. The history of the Cathar period is becoming well-known through the works of authors such as Dan Brown in the *Da Vinci Code* or Kate Mosse in *Labyrinth*. There are still traces of the period along with an increasing mythology of the events. Carcassonne is the centre of Cathar history and was the scene of a major battle. The old town has been reconstructed to reflect eleventh century life in Languedoc and many buildings date from this period. Walking through Carcassonne in March provides a glimpse of the hardships of people during the Cathar era.

The long told story of a key Cathar battle is the arrival of French General, Simon de Montfort at the outskirts of Beziers asking the bishop how the Catholic population of Beziers can be differentiated from the Cathars. The apparent response was "Kill them all, God will know his own" and with that the massacre of 20,000 inhabitants of Beziers took place.

> The *ruelles* (small streets) of Beziers were the
> center of the city in the eleventh century. We
> spent the morning exploring the tiny corkscrew
> streets in an attempt to understand what life must

have been like during this time. The cathedral of Saint Nazaire was open and we went inside to explore with the austere walls and the cold, dark stone creating a stark contrast to the sunny plaza outside overlooking the marketplace. To escape the chill, we found a nearby restaurant and descended down the narrow steps to the lower level.

Here we were seated in the former vault of the house. The area was able to hold 8 small tables that encouraged rubbing elbows with your neighbours. As we reviewed the menu and translated the details for our guests, adjoining diners bid us welcome and asked where we were from. This initiated an amusing bilingual conversation about our country and France. Many had visited Canada and as is often the case, wondered if we knew "their second cousin who lives in Montreal". Coming from the west coast of Canada, this resulted in an explanation of the vastness of the country. Following our usual two hour lunch, we continued our tour of the area. The streets are cobblestone and barely the width of a small car. Conversation was frequently interrupted when we had to jump onto a house stoop to allow a car to pass. We contrasted the reality of our situation with that of the people who lived here 800 years ago, walking these streets and living in these buildings. What must it have been like when the "streets ran red with the blood of the Cathar martrys"? We realized how this perspective of previous times provides a reality that no museum can offer. This is what March provides—without tourists, with only the local residents, one is able to follow more closely in footsteps of the past.

Even in our village there is evidence of Simon de Montfort's unwelcome visit. The small wall next to Monique's house is known as "La Brêche". This is where history indicated he broke through the town wall and massacred the villagers. As in many small villages throughout the world, house numbers and street names are replaced with historical references. Monique told us how she is known in the village as "Monique dc la Brêche" because of her families' continued occupation of the house next to the breech.

∞

In the Pyrenees, remnants of several Cathar strongholds exist in Queribus, Montsegur and Peyrepertuse. One nearby village that has captured the imagination of many is Rennes-Le Chateau with many hints of it being the secret hiding place of the riches from the Cathar strongholds. All of these sites provide an easy route for exploring although the winding roads can be tricky in winter weather. While several of the Cathar strongholds are long forgotten, there are numerous ones that are still vibrant towns and villages. Minerve, in the Aude valley, is a medieval village surrounded on three sides by rivers and steep-sided rock cliffs on all sides, providing a natural defense from invaders. The town was strategically significant during the Cathar period and became the target of one of Simon de Montfort's most protracted battles.

Our weekly French history course with a local professor was expanding both our French and our understanding of the complexities, intrigues and continued impact of the Cathar period. He intertwined historical facts with anecdotes of the time. In addition to classes, he offered personalized guided tours to various parts of Languedoc. The class set off early one cool, windy Tuesday on a field trip to Minerve located in the foothills of the Montagne Noire in the heart of the Minervois wine region. From a distance, the view of the village was breathtaking as it perched in isolation high above the river valley. Minerve is closed to cars and the walk over the bridge into the village provided the opportunity to examine how difficult the battle would have been to capture the village. Today, the only battle is for parking spots and locating the best seat in the many restaurants.

∞

Warm spring days bring the "swallows" back to Languedoc-both the feathered and the two-legged kind. With the arrival of the tiny bugs in the afternoon air, we start to see the first of the swallows arriving from Africa. As the sun begins to set, the sudden appearance of these insect catchers heralds the beginning of nighttime. They swoop and dive on the air currents above us and as night approaches, huddle in the rock face behind us.

The two-legged swallows swoop down on low-cost airlines from England and Germany to chase away the rainy blues of northern Europe. In some villages, they can be heard in the cafes and bars mingling with their French neighbours but there are some small villages that are slowly being overtaken by these temporary dwellers. If you need an "English fix", best to head to the nearest bars and cafes during the village markets.

Monique and I headed out to the market and as we came around the corner, two older men were struggling to lift a table down over a balcony from the second floor to the terrace below. This was clearly an accident waiting to happen, if not a heart attack in the making. We ran over to offer assistance and four of us maneuvered the table into position. On one side we heard "merci" and on the other side the expression was "thanks, mate". It turned out that Rupert had just arrived from Cambridge to celebrate his seventieth birthday with his neighbours who had orga-nized the daylong celebration fete. Immediately, although we did not even realize that an English person lived in our *quartier* (neighbourhood), we were invited to return for lunch and stay for the afternoon festivities. The party evolved over the course of the afternoon and evening as old and new friends and neighbours drifted in and out of the courtyard. One of the enjoyable aspects of being in Languedoc in March is there are enough "swallows" to make life interesting and to have the chance to speak English. These spontaneous happenings are open to both visitors and locals who want to get connected with life here in Languedoc.

∞

The off-season can present both challenges and opportunities for securing accommodations. While many of the seaside resorts will be shut tight and camping is not that pleasant at this time, there are numerous possibilities still available. France has an extensive network of *gites* (holiday homes) for short stay renting and many of them are available year-round. The organization Gites de France is the official body that oversees the gite system. The accommodations are typically government-inspected units that are located in villages and countryside. They may be an outbuilding on a chateau or a room in a house. In recent years, the regional government is offering financial support to homeowners to update their houses to meet the needs of the increasing tourist population. Another rental possibility is *chambers d'hotes* (B&B) which include breakfast or even *table d'hotes* (accommodation, breakfast and dinner included). The dinner is usually a set menu and may even be taken with the family. All towns and even villages of a certain size offer hotel rooms with off-season rates. Motels in the North American model are not common in France but there are a few chains often located just off the autoroutes near major cities. There are fine for a quick overnight enroute to somewhere else. If the village is very small, the Mairie often knows of someone reputable with a room to rent. For longer-term rentals, there are numerous, helpful English and French websites. The newest player on the rental block is Airbnb where people offer all sorts of rental possibilities. In France, any restaurant that calls itself an Auberge, must provide overnight accommodation. We have found these in very small towns and typically, both the meals and the rooms are very good value. In many cities and towns, the American chain, Best Western, has been transforming old hotels into very nice, modern, reasonably priced accommodations. Except for the month of August, we have never had a problem finding last minute accommodation anywhere in Languedoc. It does help to have some French to negotiate the details when working with a French rental company. The main consideration is often personal preference however, there will likely be sufficient choice to meet every need.

∞

Signs of spring in Languedoc seems to happen overnight when the warmth of the sun brings out all the buds and first fruits of the region. Strawberries, asparagus, ciboule onions, mushrooms and fresh herbs are all making their appearance.

> There it was-the sign, "asperges à vendre" that I had seen tucked by the door all winter, now swinging boldly from the doorframe. The fresh village asparagus was ready! Madame had picked this morning and we found ourselves with several

other people, waiting our turn. Monique told me how this first asparagus is her marker for the true arrival of spring. Madame asked what kind and sizes I would like and proceeded to make her selections. When I indicated that the asparagus would make a wonderful cream soup, she added the ends of the morning's pickings to my bag.

The next day, on our weekly hike into various surrounding hillsides, we came across the first shoots of wild asparagus peaking out along the sides of the old pathways. We quietly gathered enough spears for the evening's meal and like Hansel and Gretel, marked the path to aid in a return visit.

At the vegetable market, there was another surprise awaiting us-the *fraises des garrigues* had arrived. These small wild strawberries are a welcome sight after the large, berries imported from Spain and Morocco. The garrigue refers to the wild scrubby bushes in the foothills of the Montagne Noire. The dry terrain is ideal for developing the intense flavours of so many foods native to the area such as wild thyme, rosemary, lavender, honey, berries and wild game.

∞

There is a new sign of spring in Languedoc and that is the appearance of fields of plastic covered rows of melons. Languedoc is transitioning from reducing their dependence on grape growing. Farmers are ripping out the old Aramon and Carignan grapevines in favour of Merlot and Cabernet Sauvignon. They are also searching for new ways to remain on the land. A local family has capitalized on the long, hot growing season and is now transforming the southern Languedoc into a sea of melons. While at first sight, the rows of plastic are a bit disconcerting, especially after having become used to seeing the fields of vines, there is a beauty to the gently fluttering rows of white spanning the low horizon. This farming transition speaks to the hardiness and adaptability of these people who are so passionately connected to their terroir. As they have demonstrated over the centuries, it is better to adapt to changing times than leave.

∞

Visits to the weekly market never fail to astonish me as I change to such a different food-buying experience. I have discovered that there are two ways of approaching the weekly market: know what recipes you want to make and let the vendors make the correct selections or ask what is fresh or new and be prepared for quick menu changes.

Today, I need to purchase ingredients for one of this month's menu selections, "Blanquette de Veau". When I explained to Monique that I am not familiar with the cuts of meat in France and therefore asked her what cut of meat to buy, her response was quintessentially French: "Tell the butcher that you want veal for an excellent blanquette de veau. He will provide just the cut you need to ensure success."

Our Thursday village market typically has four butchers who specialize in different meats: there is the Charcuterie with his incredible variety of pork items-numerous sausages and cured meats, various pork cuts, prepared dishes that use every part but the "oink" including jellied pigs feet, snout, tongue, blood pudding and head cheese. Given the line-up at his wagon, this is a popular butcher. Monique explained that people in France say that all parts of the pig are good to eat, "de la tete à la queue, tous ce mange" (from the head to the tail, everything is eaten). She also explained that the word barbecue comes from the French expression "barbe à queue" (from whiskers to tail) and relates to cooking a whole pig on a spit in an open fire.

The next van provides the beef, lamb and veal for the village. When I ask for ground beef, known here as "steak hache", the butcher's son grinds the meat in front of my eyes with not a white Styrofoam tray in sight. When I make my request for an excellent blanquette de veau, he confers with his father and chooses a large piece of veal that he proceeds to cut into cubes. Before finishing the task, he asks how many people will be at dinner and then adds a few more pieces. This is all wrapped up in brown paper and handed to me with a "Bonne Fin Semaine" (good weekend).

The third butcher specializes in *volaille* such as chickens, guinea fowl, ducks, pigeons and small birds that I don't recognize. Most of the choices are live birds and as I watched an elderly woman make her selection, the butcher then calmly twisted the neck and gutted the bird for her. Talk about your fresh purchases. He then asked if she would like the bird prepared and she indicated, "No, I will do it myself". I vaguely remembered my mother pulling and searing pinfeathers from chickens over 50 years ago and I suspect that is part of what this woman will be doing this afternoon. As I made my choice of a large chicken hanging from a hook by his beak, I was pleased to see that I would not have to witness his demise. However, in order to ensure that I was purchasing a chicken and not some questionable fowl, he still had some feathers, beak and feet. After asking how I wanted it prepared, the butcher removed these parts before packaging the rest and sending me on my way.

The last butcher's sign said "Chevaline" meaning horsemeat. For visitors from North America this can be a squeamish choice however as Monique says, the meat is very lean, tasty and makes a wonderful stew. Part of the magic of shopping at the weekly markets is that it is easy to participate actively in a lifestyle that has been present for centuries. Friends greet each other, the merchants typically have funny comments to make and always a thank you or "bonne journée" (good day). As I thanked the butcher for my purchase, his response was "C'est moi qui vous remercie" (It is I who thank you).

∞

By early March, we begin that lovely French custom of lunch on the terrace in the noon sunshine. In France, the tendency is to have one's main meal at noon in order that the body can digest properly and women can "keep their regime" (diet). The warmer temperatures in southern Languedoc lend themselves nicely to this habit. Here are four March recipes to celebrate outdoor eating on the terrace.

BLANQUETTE DE VEAU (VEAL STEW)

This recipe signifies the arrival of spring and can be made with either veal or lamb.

Ingredients for 4 persons:

2 pounds veal, cubed

2 cooking onions, peeled but whole

2 carrots, peeled and cut into thick coins

6 whole cloves of garlic

1 cup dry white wine

1 bay leaf

2 whole cloves

2 tablespoons fresh thyme or 1 tablespoon dried

Salt & pepper to taste

⅓ cup butter

¼ cup flour

1 cup meat broth

2 egg yolks

Juice of 1 lemon

Preparation:

Step 1: can make the day before serving

Enough water to cover the ingredients

Place meat and other ingredients in a large Dutch oven and cover with water. Bring to a low boil on stove top and cook for at least 1 hour or until meat is tender and flakes easily with a fork. Chill overnight.

Step 2: Within 1 hour of serving

⅓ cup butter

¼ cup flour

1 cup meat broth

Bring meat dish to a low boil and remove onions, thyme and bay leaf.

Melt butter over low heat and stir in flour until smooth paste. Add meat broth and simmer until you have a semi-thick paste. Add to meat mixture and stir gently. Either keep in Dutch oven or transfer to heat proof, covered serving dish and keep warm.

Step 3: Prepare just before you are ready to serve

2 egg yolks

Juice of 1 large lemon

Meat broth

Stir yolks until smooth and add lemon juice until blended. In small amounts, add meat broth to mixture. This prevents curdling. Once stirred, then add mixture to Dutch oven and stir in gently.

Serve with steamed rice, new local asparagus, green salad and lots of bread to soak up the wonderful sauce. Dessert could be the first frais des garrigues. If you enjoy bubbly wines, a Blanquette de Limoux would be a lovely crisp addition with the Blanquette de Veau.

ASPÈRGES À LA MONIQUE

In France, it is common to see two types of asparagus in the markets: the white, pale looking asparagus from the north of France and the hardy, green ones from the south. There is some distain from local French housewives regarding the pale stalks as they are more expensive due to the growing technique and not deemed to be as flavourful. I had sent my husband along to the market to purchase the asparagus for dinner. Monique stopped him as he was making his selection and proceeded to tell him how it must be prepared. Unlike asparagus in the local supermarkets in America, these stalks were quite large. Monique explained how to peel the ends and discard only the bottom of the stalk.

Ingredients for 6 persons:

Sufficient asparagus for 5-6 stalks per person

¾ cup good olive oil

1 tbsp Dijon mustard

¼ cup white wine vinegar

Salt & Pepper to taste

Andrea Swan with Monique Guezel

Preparation:

Cut approximately ¼" off the root end of each stalk

Peel off the outside layer of each stalk up to the first joint

Rinse stalks in cold water

In a pot large enough to hold all the stalks laying flat, place enough water to cover and add ¾ teaspoon salt

Cook over medium heat until the root end, when pierced, is soft, 10-15 minutes

Remove from heat and leave to cool

Mustard Vinaigrette:

Monique's secret to a good vinaigrette is to use 3 parts oil to 1 part vinegar. Her advice is to use a good olive oil.

Whisk together the vinegar and mustard until blended.

Slowly drizzle in the olive oil, continuing to whisk together

Add salt and pepper to taste.

Let sit for at least 30 minutes so that flavours can meld

Pour modest amount over the cold asparagus just before serving.

SOUPE PROVENÇAL

Monique recommends this local recipe as ideal for a rainy March evening when the cupboard may be a bit bare or you are coming to the end of your visit in Languedoc.

Ingredients:

> 3 large potatoes
>
> 3 ripe tomatoes
>
> 1 large onion
>
> 1 large clove garlic
>
> 3-4 baguette rounds to cover the bottom of each soup bowl
>
> Salt & pepper to taste

Preparation:

Peel potatoes and cut in large pieces

Place in large pot of salted water and boil until tender

Place tomatoes in boiling water and simmer for a few minutes until skins loosen; rinse in cold water and then skin

When the tomatoes have been skinned, dice them and add to boiling potatoes.

Cook potatoes and tomatoes together for about 30 minutes

In a separate pan, sauté diced onions in olive oil-as Monique says "let them simmer until they are blonde". Continue cooking until the potatoes and tomatoes have cooked. It may be necessary to add a bit to the potato water to keep the onions moist.

At the end of 30 minutes, drain potato/tomato mixture retaining liquid.

Add onions to potato/tomato mixture and mash together

Puree mixture and add cooking water until it is the consistency you prefer. Salt and Pepper to taste. May be cooled at this point and re-heated when ready to serve.

When ready to serve, toast the baguette rounds and rub well with garlic clove or garlic could be finely diced and rubbed into toast as well.

Place rounds in bottom of soup bowels and ladle in soup.

TARTE TATIN

Tarte Tatin is one of those classic French recipes that the mere thought of scares off most cooks from even considering. However, under Monique's guidance, I learned that this is an easy recipe and sure to impress.

Cooks in Europe do not measure ingredients but weigh them. For example, a recipe will call for 100 grams of sugar rather than ½ cup. There is a clever measuring cup found in any French grocery store or cooking shop that indicates the most common ingredients and instead of indicating a liquid measure, each section indicates the weight amount. They are usually available in plastic and can make an inexpensive, unique souvenir of your travels. All the recipes here are made using one of these measuring devices and are then converted to liquid measures.

Ingredients:

1 kg of cooking apples or 4-5 large apples

½ cup butter cut into ½" cubes

⅓ cup white sugar

1 teaspoon ground cinnamon

Puff pastry

Preparation:

Preheat oven to 350°F

Peel, core and cut apples into thick slices

Roll pastry in the shape of the pan so that it will reach all edges

In a round flat pan that can go on the stove top and in the oven, place the butter and sugar, cinnamon and cook over medium high heat. Stir mixture constantly to prevent burning. Mixture will bubble, thicken and then turn golden brown after 10 minutes. At this point, watch carefully as it will burn quickly. Remove from heat as soon as the colour is dark golden but leave burner on low heat

Place apple pieces in the mixture without overlapping and place back on the burner for about 2 minutes to warm the apples

Cover mixture with pastry and tuck in the edges

Bake until top is golden brown approximately 20-30 minutes. If it looks like the sugar mixture is bubbling too much, turn off the bottom oven element and briefly turn on the broiler element to finish browning the crust.

After baking, let cool 10 minutes and the run a knife around the edges and invert onto a flat plate.

BATTU

This sauce is perfect for Tarte Tatin although I have used it on many fruit desserts.

It is so scrumptious, it could be used on almost anything where the recipe calls for whipping cream, sauce or ice cream.

Ingredients for 4 persons:

1 cup plain yogurt

1 cup crème fraiche

$\frac{1}{2}$ cup whipping cream

$\frac{1}{2}$ cup sugar

1 tablespoon liqueur such as Cognac, Calvados, Kirsch

Preparation:

Blend all ingredients together in a glass or ceramic bowl and let stand in refrigerator for at least 1 hour before serving.

APRIL

walking, spiritual journeys, toilettes,
festivals, cheeses, bread

April in Languedoc is bursting with life as the wisteria,
roses, vines are all suddenly covering the stone walls and fences
with a riot of colour. This is a great month to visit if you want
to see the promise of new beginnings, experience new and old
traditions and are keen on hiking and outdoor exploration.

Almost nothing reminds us of Languedoc more that the plane trees lining so many of the smaller roads of the area, especially along the Canal du Midi. Beginning around 1810, these tall, majestic trees were first planted along the marching routes of Napoleon's army in order to shade the soldiers. Today about 40,000 of them grace the banks of the Canal to shade boat travelers lazily motoring along. However, in the past several years, many of the trees have become infected with a fungus and these are being cut down to prevent further infestation.

> We were heading out of Montagnac up into the hills towards St. Guilhem. As we turned onto the road to Gignac, before us lay a stretch of canopy that dissolved into infinity. We drove for several kilometers through these magical tunnels of huge, towering tree trunks on either side with their leafy cover protecting us from the noon sun. It was easy to become distracted as one was drawn into the perspective of the tiny beam of light so far ahead of us.

Driving out into the countryside in Languedoc is always a treat whether you are encountering the alleys of plane trees, the scrub bushes of the garrigue or maguis or the umbrella pine forests of the Haute Languedoc. April is an ideal time for walking, hiking and biking in Languedoc. France has mapped out the entire country into a series of hiking and walking routes. These Grand Randonées are managed by the French Hiking Federation (FFR) and the trails are maintained and signposted by local volunteers. Whether you are a casual hiker or a committed one, it is always best to purchase official GR maps of the area or one of the Topoguide books written for the region that outline numerous walks and hikes geared to a variety of interests and skills. Many of the trails are ancient travel routes or in the backcountry, local shepherds' routes. During WW11, these routes were used by the members of the resistance groups to evade capture by the German army.

On a warm April Sunday, after a leisurely lunch in a nearby village we set out for Topoguide PR walk 27 around the Cirque de Moureze. There are several natural limestone Cirques in Languedoc that are geological formations carved out over time by the action of the water and carbon dioxide. Many of them are over one kilometer in depth. This one is located close to the village of Moureze, west of Clermont-l'Herault. As we approached the village of Moureze, there was a stark monument with numerous white crosses located at the junction approaching the village. We stopped to investigate and discovered that this memorial commemorated the capture and slaughter of 104 members of the resistance group, Maquis Bir Hakeim. Monique explained that this group of resistance fighters were known for their daring, their ability to move quickly and their military precision. They were also known for the tragedies they suffered at the hands of the German army. Walking through the maquis, the dense scrub brush that grows on the limestone hills, we could not help but think of the lives of

Andrea Swan with Monique Guezel

these young men and women scrambling about these hills. We found ourselves walking through rough, narrow canyon walls as we made our way to the edge of the Cirque. If one can imagine a huge circular area resembling a parabolic dish, this is what the cirque looks like. As we proceeded down the stone path, the wind was whistling through the crevasses and catching us as we turned through the snake-like path. Finally, we found ourselves perched on the edge looking down, way, way down to the small river meandering through the green landscape below. The Cirque de Moureze is spectacular for the vast collection of limestone spires. Unlike the Cirque de Navacelles that is located nearby, one must descend by the paths carved out of the scrub and shale. The beauty of the Cirque lies in the rough natural formations and harsh conditions.

One note of caution when walking out in the forests or scrublands in the Languedoc. There are several critters that can pose problems to the unsuspecting hiker. There are forests of umbrella pines that house nests of caterpillars in March and April. These caterpillars hatch in the spring and can be found crawling along the roadways and byways. They are very interesting to watch as they crawl along one in front of the other, nose to tail forming long lines. They secrete a powerful chemical that can cause severe burning and blistering on skin if any form of contact is made, including touching the ground or surfaces they may have touched. Even dogs are at risk with these insects. While more prevalent during the summer months, vipers, scorpions and wild boar can be found in the dry brush and can present serious risk. Hikers are advised to keep covered and to avoid walking in the early evening.

∞

It is interesting to visit another country to see how it handles social problems and issues compared to one's own country. We have learned that during the Depression years, France addressed the unemployment problem by intentionally building vast networks of roads across the country. This economic policy kept young men employed and prepared France for the emerging post-war economy. We now see a similar approach being taken again as the country pours money into upgrading and replacing various aspects of its infrastructure. Just as highways replaced rail lines, the regional government has begun developing a series of *"voies vertes"* (green ways) replacing unused rail lines with biking and walking trails. These are being constructed all through Languedoc and will eventually provide a complete network of criss-crossing trails throughout the region. With a maximum two percent grade, they open up a completely new opportunity for *en plein air* (outdoors) activities.

The Grande Randonées from Bedarieux to Mazemet, running through the spectacular countryside of the Cevennes, was well outside our scope of hiking prowess. However, when we saw the newly completed voie verte, "PassaPais", we took a chance and started out. The route is gentle and requires little effort, even on the uphill return. We passed through villages that were off the beaten highway track but provided accommodation as needed because of their former connection to the rail line. Along the way, we met afternoon walkers, families with their young children on tricycles and older people being pushed in wheelchairs and even a man walking his donkey as part of a pilgrimage through the Cevennes. At various stops, we moved away from the trail and went into towns to explore further. It is always a pleasure for us to discover well kept gastronomic and artistic secrets in these out of the way places.

∞

As France works to promote secularism, it is interesting to see the renaissance of spiritual and religious growth in France and particularly in Languedoc. Perhaps because of ancient roots of religious tolerance that allowed the Cathars to flourish and Jews to be welcomed, the *Camisards* (Huguenots) to find safety and acceptance, Languedoc is again home to a revival of diverse religious and spiritual expression. Many of the abbeys and monasteries destroyed during the revolution are now being re-populated by a new generation of monks and nuns, offering programs and housing to those who seek spiritual renewal.

While many of the abbeys and monasteries are reclaiming their function as places of spiritual and religious growth, some such as Abbaye de Fondfroide, near Narbonne, are worth a visit because they are such well-preserved examples of a previous life in Languedoc. New Catholic religious centers are being nurtured in Languedoc as well as a revitalization of the old. La Famille de St. Joseph is a new order of Catholic religious founded in 1990. Following the rule of St. Benoit, this order is building a large monastery in the small village of Puimisson and is dedicated to providing respite to those who seek retreat from a busy world.

For a study of the Protestant religions in southern France, one only has to visit the Cevennes to gain an understanding of the history of this period. The main focus that evokes this history is Alès in the Cevennes and the Mas Soubeyan at Mialet. The Mas was known as the human hiding-place. The museum now illustrates the way of life of Protestant communities between the Revocation of the Treaty of Nantes in 1685 and the Edict of Tolerance in 1787 when persecution and expulsion were common. Anduze lies at the gateway to the Cevennes and features the largest "*temple*" (Protestant worship house) in France with the austere façade reflecting the restrained approach to Huguenot life during the Wars of Religion. Monique shared the story of her father being posted to a small town in the Cevennes and commenting on all the well-kept small stone monuments in the back gardens of the houses. He later learnt that these were gravestones and that family members were buried on family plots because they were not allowed a communal graveyard.

Outside a small village near Lodeve, lies the Buddhist monastery and retreat centre of Lerab Ling. This spiritual center of Buddhism in Europe offers programs and retreats for a wide range of participants.

> More out of curiosity than anything, Monique and I travelled to Lerab Ling to see for ourselves what people were talking about. While the Oriental building and landscaping designs seemed out of place in the hilly terrain of the Cevennes, the focus as a retreat centre was very much in keeping with the quiet and isolation of the region. As we walked about the monastery grounds, we chatted about how Languedoc has, over the centuries, been a breeding ground for spiritual renewal; this is seen in the development of the Cathar theology then the Huguenots and now various new forms of spiritual expression.

If combining spiritual growth and wine is your passion, then the Monestère de Solan near Uzes is worth a visit. In 1992, eight women from the Greek Orthodox church bought an abandoned farm and begun the Monestère de Solan, dedicating themselves to following the Byzantine rite and living out the Orthodox belief that just as humans need time and help to grow to their full potential, so too does the earth. Today, a small community of nuns provides hospitality for anyone visiting, attending retreats or helping out in their *bio* (organic) vineyards and kitchens to produce a wide variety of wines, jams and incense.

In the middle ages until the expulsion in 1394, both Beziers and Pezenas had flourishing Jewish communities and Beziers was known as Le Petit Jerusalem because it was such an important center of Judaism. Today, the communities are small and the synagogue in Beziers is hidden behind closed doors near the Cathedral St Madeleine.

In times past, France colonized many Islamic countries and gave full French citizenship to these populations. As the result, France has welcomed people from a wide range of Islamic cultures. In most cases, because of the secular expectations of French culture, people quietly practise their faith or have assimilated into French life. Most towns and cities will have a mosque that is the center of cultural life, particularly for new arrivals.

∞

April is often the season for Easter and although France is officially a secular country with no official religion, festivals and pageants continue to mark the events. This is particularly the case in the western, where the Catalan culture continues to influence the festivals of the region. The main Easter spectacle is called La Sanch and is reminiscent of the Easter pageant in Seville. Perpignan, Collioure and Arles les Tech carry out a Good Friday tradition started in 1416 by the Dominicans. In centuries past, Good Friday was the typical day for executions and the procession that snaked through the town or village was to support those on their way to the gallows. The condemned wore a long, black garment with a pointed hood. While today the procession does not include the condemned, red and black garments are worn. The red signifies the supporters and black represents the condemned. On their shoulders, they carry the Misteris, life-sized representations of the Passion and they parade solemnly through the streets to the rhythm of local historical chants.

∞

For a more upbeat Easter celebration, the *Toques et Clochers* festival near Limoux offers a chance to sample the special wines of the region. In the middle ages, a Dominican monk discovered that his wine had fermented in an interesting manner, producing an effervescent effect. He then travelled to the Champagne region and re-created the effect that is now the famous Champagne wines. At least that is the story told by the winemakers in the Limoux region as they market the wonderful Blanquette de Limoux. To raise the profile of its famous beginnings, the Toques et Clochers gastronomic festival, held on the Palm Sunday weekend celebrates the unique foods and wines of the region. Each year a different small village is chosen to host the celebrations. The focus is on the wine and the foods of the Limoux region as chefs wearing their *toques* (chef's hats) prepare specialties. The money raised is used by the village to repair or restore the *clochers* (steeples) of the village churches. The pairing of the food and religion is a time-honoured tradition that is evidently being repackaged for modern era.

∞

April is a good time to combine walking and hiking with the spiritual growth of a pilgrimage. The famous pilgrimage routes to Santiago de Compostela have many beginnings in France and several pass through Languedoc. The Arles route is located totally within Languedoc, visiting Montpellier, St.

Guilhem le désert, Lodeve, Castres, and Toulouse before joining up with the other four routes at St. Jean Pied de Port. The route offers the chance to visit large cities, small villages and scrubby, sparsely populated hilly terrain in between. Friends who have done both the French and Spanish routes have indicated that the accommodation and meals on the French routes are better, less crowded and more conducive to a leisurely pace.

We did not intend to complete the whole route but instead met friends in a hamlet in the high Languedoc and joined them as they walked the Arles route. The warmth of the sun melted away any aches as we walked slowly through the narrow confines of the old path. It was not difficult walking and we spent our time in silence or quiet conversation. During the 15 kilometer journey, we came across other people who shared information with us regarding the track ahead. By noon, we ambled into the village and into the local Auberge where the *plat de jour* (daily special) was more than enough to hold us for the remainder of the day. We quickly learned that it was important to plan your day so that the bulk of your day's journey is finished by the time you stop for lunch. The hardy lunch paired with the local wine made for a need for a siesta. Even in April, the warm sun soon lulls you to sleep. By mid afternoon, we were ready for our final few kilometers and easily made it to our destination. In April it is possible to simply show up at hotel and auberges at the end of the afternoon but it is important to plan a reasonable itinerary to ensure that there are cafes, auberges and hotels along your daily walking routes.

In 1878, Robert Louis Stevenson set out on a twelve-day journey of discovery through the Cevennes along with his little donkey, Modestine. However, she proved to be a challenging travel companion. There are opportunities today to repeat the journey through the Cevennes but it would be worth reading "Travels with a Donkey in the Cevennes" before considering the trip as donkeys can present unique learning opportunities.

∞

Whatever time of the year you might focus on the walking, hiking or pilgrimage routes of Languedoc, there is an added feature that can make an interesting additional highlight to your visit and that's the *toilettes* (bathrooms) of France. Especially in the Haute Languedoc where there are fewer tourists, the plumbing may not have quite caught up to modern standards. This makes for an adventure as one tries to figure out exactly how to access the facilities, how to contort ones body into the space and how the plumbing works. Building codes likely did not exist or else people didn't bother conforming to the codes. This makes for interesting design features and great photographs.

We recently decided to add a second bathroom to our ancient house and engaged Gael, our local handy man to prepare the plans. As the house is of unknown age and built into the side of the town rampart, previous building plans are non-existent. Therefore, we engaged in the time honoured method of investigating how any new plumbing would be joined to the pre-existing lines. As soon as my husband and Gael were outside examining the cobblestone walkway up to the house, other neighbours appeared magically to offer advice. Before long, seven males, including two young boys, were conferring on how the pipes ran through the rockwork. Before long, iron rods were out and water covers were off for the group to peer down. In the end, it was decided that the best way was to take a jack-hammer and break up some concrete to determine where the current lines could possibly be running. Of course, there is the possibility that we could uncover an underground vault as the hillside is peppered with old, forgotten, medieval caves and tunnels that were often used as escape routes. In all likelihood, most of the toilettes found in the Haute Languedoc were built with this same collaborative method as people tried to find ways to add "modern" indoor plumbing to pre-existing ancient houses.

∞

At least since the time of the Cathars and the famous ballad, "*Chanson de Rolland*", Languedoc has fostered and supported artists and writers. April is a great time to uncover the talents of new and old writers, singers, dancers and artists. Many of these people are transplants from other countries who prefer the climate, both weather and community support, to foster their creative talents. There are numerous exhibitions, *concours* (competitions) and festivals in April throughout Languedoc. The coastal towns and villages are focusing efforts on becoming internationally known centers of artistic and musical excellence. Beginning with the villages along the Cote Vermeille at the western edge of the region and running along to Montpellier, there are an increasing number of art galleries and musical possibilities. As well, there may often be opportunities to meet your favourite artist or writer in his or her village bar. While Montpellier and Carcassonne are major centers for the arts, there are many smaller towns and villages that focus on being centers for a specific artistic style, literary genre or dance technique. Lodeve has been a center of artistic influence since the late 1700s and is now well known for the major art exhibitions it holds each year. Montpellier, as the largest city in the region, is home to the Opera, major dance companies and numerous art galleries. Sete and Agde, although small cities, are focusing on becoming destinations for emerging artists. Even villages, such as Roujan and Lagrasse foster artistic events by hosting high caliber choirs, artist exhibitions and dance performances throughout the year. Several of these communities feature weeklong festivals throughout the spring and summer. The Dance Festival in Montpellier is a must see event for serious dance enthusiasts.

Friends invited us to Montpellier to see an Israeli dance troupe perform. Off we went for this first-time visit to the Corum, Montpelier's performing arts and conference centre. Having visited both opera houses in Paris, the Vienna opera house and others in Canada, we assumed that Montpellier, having a smaller population, would be quaint and provincial. Bad assumption, it was incredible. From the modern design, to the walls of loges, the experience was unique. One felt so close to the dancers only to realize that there were 2000 other people also watching and probably feeling just as connected. As the schedule of upcoming events revealed, Montpellier is connected to so much of Europe, the Middle East and Africa and therefore attracts both emerging and established artists from all over the world.

Shortly after this visit, we attended the newly renovated theatre in Pezenas and were overwhelmed at the beauty of this small space. The Belle Époque architecture had been completely restored to its former grandeur, complete with loges. One felt completely out of place in modern attire!

∞

President Charles De Gaulle apparently said that is was impossible to govern a country that produced 246 different cheeses. Were he to say that today, it would be over 500 varieties and April is an ideal time to discover many of the local varieties especially the chevre and fromages de Larzac. Just as with wine, France has established clear rules about cheese production and has designed a grading system similar to the Appellation system used for wine. Languedoc is justly famous for several internationally known cheeses such as Roquefort, Chevre, Pelardon, Cathare, and the sheep cheeses from the Pyrenees. Because so many of these cheeses never find their way onto North American store shelves, now is the time to explore to your heart's content. Many of the artisan cheese makers provide tours and opportunities to visit the farms. As well, more and more people are making their own small batch cheeses for sale at the farm gate or at local markets.

> I can remember my father, a former cheese maker in Canada, in awe of the blue cheese from Roquefort. As I child, I certainly did not appreciate the green veins running through the white, crumbly cheese. If it didn't say KRAFT, it wasn't cheese. After many visits to France, I came to appreciate the variety and richness of the cheeses. On Monique's advice, one day in April, we made our way up into the hills to Roquefort, about one hour from our home, to pay homage to this special cheese. After leaving the autoroute, we followed the small signs that indicated the way to the hamlet of Roquefort sur Soulzon. Given the renown of Roquefort cheese, we expected to see a large village not this small hamlet as the site of one of the world's great cheeses. This hamlet is perched on the side of the limestone caves

of the high Larzac mountains. There are three main producers to visit in the hamlet and they all offer tours. The secret to Roquefort cheese lies in the curing rooms deep inside the caves. The limestone caves have been carved by wind and rain over the centuries creating fine wind tunnels throughout. It is through this ventilation system and the spores present in the caves that the cheeses are inoculated with the bacteria that grows the blue pockets in the cheeses.

The first mention of this process was in 79AD and the myth that surrounds the cheese is that a young shepherd, tending his herds near the mouth of the cave, saw a beautiful girl in the distance and leaving his bread and ewes milk cheese, went to meet her. When he returned, the cheese was transformed into a delicious cheese that won the girl's heart. After a visit to the caves, perhaps, you too will discover this magical potion.

Mas Rolland, located near the hamlet of Montesquieu, is a small farm with a growing reputation for producing excellent *chevre* (goat cheese). Like so many of the small farmers in Languedoc, this family is returning to the old ways. Some producers have lived here for generations and others are newcomers from many regions and countries. They are all committed to small-scale production emphasizing the local environment.

∞

Not many countries have fought a war over bread but that was a key reason for the French revolution and ever since, the price and availability of bread is dictated by the government. The classic French baquette conjures up not only an image of an old man on a bicycle with his baquette in the panier but it is also a symbol of equality (pain d'egalite) in that citizens must have access to reasonable priced bread. Today, not only must a baker produce a baquette that is made from a specific recipe and cost no more than 85 centimes ($1.20) but the municipal police determine when the baker can close the shop as people must have access to bread every day of the week. Each one of the three bakeries in our village has a designated day off and they must all open on Sunday morning until noon and any state holidays, including Christmas. The hard won right to have fresh bread is not taken lightly in this country.

Besides the traditional baguette, French boulangeries and patisseries are a treasure trove of delicacies. After featuring all the hiking and walking possibilities for the month of April, it seems only natural that one would reward oneself with the search for the perfect baguette, mille feuilles or Paris Brest. When visiting bakeries it is best to note if it is run by an independent baker or a chain. Like wine, cheese and so many other foods, bakeries must comply with strict regulations to earn the use of the words Boulanger or Boulangerie in the title of the store. If the store name does not contain these words, then there is a good chance that the items have been made offsite and baked locally or even made completely in a commercial factory. Like so many other aspects of France life, the commitment to high standards of food and wine production ensure that the ways of the past are less likely to disappear quickly. Often, the boulangerie will gain a reputation for particular items. Why not add to your memories by doing your own research on who makes the best *pain aux raisens*, baguette, *pain de campagne* or *festive*.

∞

As Monique and I chose recipes for April, we were reminded that this is the month of transition-some products are reaching their peak while others are beginning to appear at the markets. France seems to pay attention to seasonal products and it gives us an opportunity to try new items rather than rely on the year-round availability of products.

GRATIN D'ASPÈRGES ET JAMBON

Monique shared this recipe as it is a favourite of her son, Phillipe. With the asparagus at its peak, it is a good spring recipe. In preparing this recipe, Monique cautioned me about adding salt as the jambon de la montagne tends to be quite salty. She also shared with me the origins of "Fleur de Sel", the expensive salt currently hitting the gourmet shops in North America. She said how her mother-in-law in Brittany would go out in the early morning after a calm sea and lightly skim off the fine salt crystals forming on the salt flats. These are prized by good cooks as they have higher mineral content than normal table salt. She felt that she had been accepted when she received a gift of this special salt from her mother-in-law.

Ingredients for 4-6 persons:

2 large slices of thinly shaved ham per person-Monique uses a "jambon de la montagne" which would be similar to prosciutto or ham shaved from a cured ham rather than cooked ham from a package

6-8 asparagus spears per person

1 cup crème fraiche to which you have added ¼ cup cream or milk

½ cup grated Emmenthal or Gruyere cheese

Salt and pepper to taste

Preparation:

Pre-heat over to 350°F

Cut the ham slices in half making sure that you can roll the asparagus spears in the smaller slices

Peel the ends of the asparagus to remove any hard or woody bits from the stalks

Tightly roll 3-4 asparagus spears in each piece of ham and lay side by side in a flat casserole dish

Pour crème fraiche mixture over the rolled spears, sprinkle the cheese over top and add salt and pepper

Bake for approximately 30 minutes until cheese in bubbly and golden

SALAD FRISÉE

In France, there are several ways of serving salad, each with their own "rules". Some restaurants will feature salads as a separate section. Beware that these are not starters but full meals containing a variety of vegetables and protein sources.

Salads may be served as a starter course and they are likely to feature cheese, egg or cured meat. Not as large as a *plat* (main course) salad, they can certainly take the edge off your appetite. Finally, a small greens only salad may follow the main course and is considered a palate cleanser to settle the stomach, aid digestion and foster the transition between the main dish and the cheese course. In all cases, the salad dressing is typically a simple vinaigrette made from scratch.

In preparing the salad, Monique revealed yet another of her tricks. Rather than search for a garlic press as what self-respecting French woman has a garlic press, she pressed a fork into the side of the mixing bowl and grated the clove of garlic across it. Voila, finely minced garlic.

This recipe uses Salad Friseée, a curly headed variety with a slightly sharp taste.

Ingredients for 4 persons:

Head of Salad Frisée or other nutty tasting lettuce

$1/2$ cup walnut pieces

Enough slices of smoked duck breast, smoked salmon, liver paté OR prosciutto for 4 people.

Vinaigrette:

> 1 clove garlic
>
> $\frac{1}{2}$ teaspoon mustard
>
> 3 tablespoons white wine vinegar
>
> $\frac{1}{4}$ cup olive oil
>
> $\frac{1}{4}$ teaspoon black pepper
>
> $\frac{1}{4}$ teaspoon salt

Preparation:

In the salad bowl, mince the garlic clove or rub the bowl with a garlic half

Mix the mustard and vinegar and add minced garlic.

Slowly whisk in the olive oil until the ingredients are fully blended together

Add the salt and pepper.

Leave the vinaigrette in the bowl and add the salad fixings at the last minute, tossing together to coat.

PERSIMMON TARTE

Persimmons are not a well-known fruit in North America and the reason may be because you either love them or hate them. The typical varieties are either the sweet, pale orange, squat variety called Fuji or the deep orange, larger, more astringent variety called Kaki. Both varieties are available between January and June and are worth a try. In order to sweeten the Kaki, place it in the freezer for at least a few hours and this will break down the tissue, giving it a wonderful sweet taste. I often have a few on hand in the freezer for unexpected, quick treats. Either variety can be sliced and served raw as an accompaniment to paté or cheese. Otherwise, it can be used in curries, baking or drinks to impart an unusual sweet taste. This simple tarte may be an easy introduction to this versatile winter fruit.

Ingredients:

Pie crust, either made or purchased

3 persimmons-if using Kakis, make sure you have left them in the freezer for at least a few hours.

1 beaten egg

¼ cup sugar

½ teaspoon nutmeg

Pinch or salt

Pinch of cinnamon

3 tablespoons unsalted butter

Preparation:

Heat oven to 475°F.

Roll out the piecrust and place in pan. Brush with beaten egg and refrigerate for 1 hour.

Slice persimmon into equal slices or chunks, covering the piecrust.

Sprinkle with sugar, spice mixture and cut in butter.

Bake for 30 minutes until fruit is firm and pastry golden.

Serve with crème fraiche or Battu.

MAY

transhumance, prehistoric remnants,
Roma, feria, mineral springs

May offers the opportunity to participate in several special Languedoc festivals. The *transhumance*, the moving of herds from the lowlands to the highlands, the spring *feria* (bull-fighting festival) and the Roma festival honouring St Sarah, known as the handmaiden of the three Marys, Mary Magdelen, Mary Salome and Mary Jacobe are good reasons to come to Languedoc in

May. May is one of the best shoulder months for travelling in Languedoc. Warm temperatures, fewer tourists but lots of open venues and attractions make this an ideal time to come.

Beginning with the first of May, the month unfolds as a tribute to much of France's history. On this day, throughout Languedoc you will see people selling bunches of Lily of the Valley, this wonderful flower that heralds the arrival of spring. In 1561, King Charles the ninth of France received a bouquet and was so pleased that every May 1st, he presented the ladies of the court with bouquets thus beginning this long tradition. Today, the bouquets are sold by groups to raise money for charities. One note of caution, the flowers are toxic, hence the reference to the old saying that they make a good eleven o'clock broth (a poisoned drink). Because May 1st is also International Workers Day, only workers organizations are permitted to sell the flowers bunches for their charities.

∞

One of the oldest practices in Languedoc is the transhumance, the moving of animals from lowlands to highlands for summer grazing. Prehistoric records indicate that goats and sheep had been domesticated as far back as 13,000 to 15,000 years ago. Some of the routes still used today follow those same ancient trails. This practice is found throughout the Mediterranean regions however, with modern faming practices, there are fewer herds moved to higher ground although there are still around 60,000 animals moved in the Pyrenees Oriental alone. The herds are made up of the sheep from numerous farms and in order to identify who owns what, the sheep are marked with coloured tassels much like cattle brand-ing in America. However these neck tassels provide a colourful addition to the parade of sheep as they are herded through the villages enroute to their summer pastures. May marks the begin-ning of the festivals and herding of goats, sheep and cows up to Mont Lozere and Mont Aigoual in the Causses of Herault and the Gard, the Cevennes in Herault and Lozere and the Pyrenees. Invariably, the beginning of the journey is marked with great celebrations and rituals. Even though modern farming tech-niques could supply sufficient feed for the animals, the trans-humance is more about preserving a way of life and ensuring that the old ways remain. For many shepherds, their days up in the hills will be spent making the specialty goat cheeses that sell in the local markets. These handmade cheeses will reflect the terroir of the region where the animals are grazing. Like any product made close to its source, these cheese delicacies will give hints of the wild thyme, lavender and rosemary of the high Causses and Cevennes. Watch for these special treats at the regional markets in the Haute Languedoc and taste the fruits of the shepherds' labours.

One special journey is taken by the black Merens horses of the Pyrenées-Orientale. These pony sized horses bear a strik-ing resemblance to horses painted in pre-historic caves in this area. They are sturdy, sure-footed animals that have survived for centuries in the unforgiving hills and mountains of the Pyrenées. They are now considered endangered and efforts are being made to protect the stock and increase numbers.

The transhumance can happen in both directions during the same time. Located on the edge of the salt marshes of the

Andrea Swan with Monique Guezel

Petit Camargue, Sommieres is a town north of Montpellier. It is the center of the upland winter-feeding grounds of the Camargue cow herds. The April festival marks the beginning of the move back down to the lowlands of the Camargue. Sommières continues the traditions, highlighting the relationship between the people and the animals of the region. Here you can see an *abrivado* (bull run) where the bulls run through the town chased by Camargue cowboys. Similar to Pamploma, people race to escape the bulls and riders. Many of the activities derive from ancient circus games and are a reflection of the early Roman influence present throughout this region.

∞

Languedoc is home to many pre-historic discoveries and many of them are easy to explore. The Aude and the Pyrenees Orientale offer both interpretation centers and actual caves to visit. Following the discovery of Tauteval Man in 1971, there has been active archeological work carried out thoughout the region. The Musée de Tauteval is considered the centre of pre-history in Europe and the activities offered are of interest to all ages. The Herault also has a large museum of pre-historical artifacts and a walking trail with dinosaur remains at Pic St Loup. The whole region was populated throughout early civilization and many left evidence in their cave paintings and implements of living. Some of the special remnants to visit are the menhirs or giant monoliths put up by unknown groups that likely date back 4000-6000 years. Some of the best are located in the Cevennes on the north west side of Mont Lozere. The walking trails are designed to give the visitor good views of these enigmatic, ancient monuments. The museum in Narbonne has an excellent collection of pre-historic remains along with their early Greek and Roman collections as does the museum in Lodeve.

∞

According to a slightly more modern legend, following the crucifixion of Jesus, Lazarous, Mary Magdelene, Mary Jacobe and Mary Salome, along with their young, black, Egyptian servant, Sarah, fled the holy land in a boat and landed on the shores of France near the mouth of the Rhone river, today named Saintes Maries de le Mer. The myth continues that Mary Magdalen went to St. Baume where she lived in a cave clothed only with her hair. Mary Salome and Mary Jacobe remained near the mouth of the Rhone and were venerated by the local people. Lazarous went to Marseille and became the first bishop. Variations on the story all lead to interesting suppositions of what happened. One theory is that the current myths have evolved from earlier, pagan myths. However, the belief came about, for the past few hundred years, the Roma community of Europe have adopted Sarah as their patron saint and celebrate her story in late May in Saintes Maries de la Mer. The shrine in the village is dedicated to Sarah and apparently, until 1912, only Roma were allowed in the crypt. For decades, May 24, 25 have marked the pilgrimage to the shrine and Roma from all over the world descend on this small fishing village.

> The throng of people made it almost impossible to move forward. The music and energy were so infectious that we had to be part of the magic.

Slowly the procession moved towards the church of St. Michael where all day long, people had been entering and placing candles around the shrine to Sarah. At the head of the procession, statues of the two Marys were carried forward as people stretched to try and touch the feet of these holy symbols. We watched, mesmerized by the fervour of the people around us. When we reached the church, the statue of Sarah was solemnly carried out, her figure blackened by the smoke of all the candles. Gently, brilliant, glittering cloaks were wrapped around her and four young Roma men moved forward to raise her onto their shoulders, the crowd shouting "Viva, Sainte Sarah". Everyone then broke into a haunting, repetitive chant. The mass of people snaked slowly through the narrow village streets following the raised statue. We were now caught up in this procession as it headed down to the sea. As we moved closer into the open area, riders on beautiful white Camargue horses, ancestors of ancient Arabian stock, moved in to provide an honour guard for the statue bearers. At the waters edge, we watched the troupe wade into the sea and submerge the statue. We recognized the local bishop and someone who was identified as the "King of the Gypsies" leading the procession. Then somehow, the mass of people turned slowly around and proceeded back into the centre of the village. The second day of the festival honours the two Marys but the atmosphere is now focused on celebrations, family reunions and music. It has been said that Roma see this festival as a time to renew and strengthen their traditions of music and family. We were therefore, not surprised on the 25th to see so many weddings happening as apparently, it brings great luck to be married during this special festival. Except for the religious ceremonies, the rest of the time is spent in a whirlwind of music, dancing and laughter. It is so easy to simply walk around and enjoy the haunting melodies and dancing that make this otherwise sleepy village come alive in May.

Roma are known by many names-*gypsies, gitanes, tziganes, gitanos, manouches.* Roma first settled throughout France in the 15th century. It is thought that those settling in Languedoc came from Spain when they were expelled as part of the Inquisition. There have been Roma communities in many of the coastal towns throughout the recent centuries. They have tended to integrate into the communities and are less likely to be part of a "traveler" tradition where people move from place to place in small groups. The latest waves of immigration were from the Spanish Civil war and now the Eastern European countries. The Roma population has been the focus of much attention over the past few years as the European borders are opened up to allow easier migration. There continues to be repression and antagonism towards Roma, especially where they have had a difficult time integrating into the communities or are poor and uneducated making them easy prey for activities such as prostitution and theft. Most of Languedoc is free from the pan handling and soliciting that is present in the large cities such as Barcelona and most Roma are trying to integrate into their communities.

France has a long tradition of supporting "travelers" and all villages over five thousand residents must provide space for the *gens de voyage*, people who travel around in caravans. These areas provide electrical and sanitation hookups and are handy for anyone travelling in a camper van. Roma are an integral part of French life and like any group of people, there will be those who give a negative reputation to a culture. That is part of life in France where the emphasis on assimilation is so engrained. Much is being done to support Roma who want to become part of the French fabric but is does mean that many of the habits they arrive with such as not wanting to school their children, are being met with government reprisals. There is a good opportunity to study how another country addresses issues similar to those in ones own country. Certainly, there are lessons to be learned.

∞

One of the major festivals in May is the *feria* (bull fight festival) in Nîmes. Held from the Wednesday before Pentecost until the following Monday, this festival draws hundreds of thousands to the city of Nîmes. The festival starts with the *pegoulade* (procession) that happens the first night with floats, musicians and dances snaking through the streets of Nîmes. The main events are the bullfights, a sport not for the faint of heart and the *corrida* (bull fight) in Nîmes follows the Spanish model where the goal is for either the bull or the matador to finish up dead, usually the bull. The Spanish form of bull fighting has been outlawed in France for a number of years but Nîmes and Arles claim it as part of their *patromonie* (heritage) and are exempt from the ban. During the feria, the corridas are held twice a day in the Roman coliseum where locals and visitors participate in this ages old blood sport eulogized by the likes of Ernest Hemingway and Jean Cocteau. As one person said, this may not be the event to take your girlfriend to! However, the audience is made up of all ages and sexes and the screams and shouts are evidence that those attending have been drawn into the enthusiasm. One special element of the feria is that often the world's most famous matadors come to Nîmes and as several of them are from France, there is particular Nimoise pride in the event. The corrida is only a small part of the excitement of the feria and the town is awash in street entertainment and *bodegas* (mini restaurants) spring up all around the city during the event. The action starts in the late afternoon and continues until late into the night. It's an exciting event that provides a glimpse into the life and culture of this city that has known bloodshed for centuries.

> One May morning, on the spur of the moment, we decided to take our guests to Nîmes, totally unaware of what awaited us. Our plan was to visit the many well-preserved Roman ruins and enjoy the quiet ambiance of this southern Languedoc town. The streets were packed, an unusual occurrence in this rather sleepy town. However, after several attempts we did find a parking space and found ourselves drawn

towards the smells and sounds of the centre ville. No matter where we looked, there were stalls selling bright, colourful Spanish and Provençal shirts, scarves and hats; artful posters announced the dates and times for the local corridas; many of the menus at the main bistros were featuring *daube de gardian* (variation of beef stew) as the plat de jour. We discovered fairly quickly that we had chosen the "Feria de Pentecote" to come. First, of course, we needed to gather our strength for the afternoon's events so we chose a bistro located in a nearby plaza and asked about the plat de jour. The young waiter informed us that during the feria, the bulls that were killed the preceding day were butchered and the meat shared among the local restaurants to be served as daube de gardian. He explained that it was an honour for a restaurant to be chosen to receive the meat from a bull that had fought valiantly and given his life. It was also important that the chef prepare a wonderful daube in recognition of the bull. Several of us chose the daube as a way of acknowledging this ritual and the link between the cultural aspects of the feria. It was delicious and sparked a heated debate on the morality of the manner in which the meat was acquired. Because meat and fish are so fresh and often such unusual cuts, we have discovered that such a discussion is often part of a French meal. After lunch, we wandered through the various markets and stopped to listen to the variety of musicians and Flamenco dancers. Because Nîmes is on the border of the Camargue, much of the music has a strong Roma flavour to it. The guitars, violins and singers create a magical backdrop to the energy of the day. As we turned the corner onto a large open area, unfolding before us was a demonstration of Camargue and Spanish horsemen dressed in traditional outfits, parading their horses through an intricate dance to demonstrate the flexibility and expertise needed to work with the bulls.

In the lazy, late afternoon sun, as we headed towards the Roman *arène* (arena), the crowds had increased and we moved shoulder to shoulder through the ruelles around the arène. The large plaza immediately surrounding the arène was thick with people heading to the main doors. The Nîmes arène is one of the best-preserved Roman forums and has been in continual operation since Roman times. While it is now often the scene of concerts, the tradition of blood sports such as bull fighting continues. Obviously, one comes prepared to attend a corrida as most people were dressed in Spanish costumes and red and black featured predominately in the color scheme. We had already decided that the corrida was not for us but participating, even peripherally, in this feria was exciting and not to be missed.

There continues to be much debate about the Spanish version of the corrida and as people voice their concern and numbers drop, changes are afoot. Most ferias, have adopted a more humane approach to the corrida in which the animal is not killed but instead the matador must retrieve ribbons attached to the bulls' horns—no mean feat when faced with an enraged bull. There are opponents of this milder version who protest the stress and fear that the animal undergoes as he is prodded to behave wildly. The corrida may be a dying tradition in France as more and more ferias are replacing the corrida with a variety of other spectacles.

For a feria of a different kind, Pezenas offers the Feria de Pentecote that focuses on the artistic past of which Pezenas is so famous. Colourful, travelling troubadours saunter throughout the tiny streets of old Pezenas and a wide variety of performances are featured throughout the feria period.

∞

If large, fearsome bulls are not of interest, there is another group of interesting animals that make their annual appearance during May. The mythological creatures that form part of the culture of Languedoc. In late May or early June, the Drac makes its appearance in the town of Beaucaire in the Gard. He is a twelfth century myth of the dragon who could make itself invisible to humans and fed on little boys and girls who strayed close to the banks of the Rhone river. Today he still causes squeals from frightened children as they carry lanterns and follow the dragon through the streets of the town.

The beast of Gevaudan first appeared in the Lozere around 1764 when a young girl was killed by a ferocious beast. Many more suspicious deaths occurred around Gevaudan and rumours circulated about a werewolf or a hyena trained by the noblemen to control the peasants. Finally, when the gruesome deaths did not abate, the clergy pronounced that a curse had descended on the region. The story has now been handed down through the generations creating its own fascination, rituals and festivals. One can now visit a museum in Saugues dedicated to the beast.

One would have to wait until June but another mythological creature of Languedoc is the Gargantua that first appeared in 1884. He is an insatiable giant whose heavy footsteps trampled the ground on which he walked. It is said that this whimsical giant created islands from the mud on his clogs, tall columns of stone in the Tarn valley are said to be the result of his work. He is seen as a friendly creature and he is celebrated with parades and feasts. As with many myths of Languedoc, they offer an excuse to get together, celebrate and eat well. If you should happen onto any of these festivals, enjoy!

∞

The Cevennes and Causses mountains offer two special treats for the traveler. The limestone caves are rich sources of mineral formations and several of these caves have been discovered over the last century. The Grotte de Clamouse was formed by water carving out caverns inside the mountain as it found its way down into the river far below. Inside the cavern, one moves from cave to cave overwhelmed by the heights and magnificence of the stalactites and stalagmites created over the millions of years. Even today, with each drop of mineral water slowly dropping from the ceilings, new formations emerge. The caves have been lit to enhance the view and commentaries suggest imaginative explanations of the formations. These same geological formations also provide another wonderful treat and that is the hot springs bubbling up through the limestone crevices. There are now numerous spas that take advantage of these thermal springs just as the Romans did centuries ago. La Chadette high on the Aubrac plain offers a cocktail of therapies. Lamalou les Bains has been a centre for *reeducation* (rehabilitation) therapies for over two hundred years and physicians still prescribe these cures for a variety of ills. In Amelie les Bains, the thermal springs offer sulphur baths that are recognized for their therapeutic benefit for rheumatoid arthritis and for lung problems. One of the facilities even features a bathing area first used by the Romans. For a slightly different spa experience, there is the Jardins St Benoit in Saint Laurent de la Cabrerisse where one can swim in their heated pool, visit the hammam for an exquisite massage and enjoy a wine tasting as well. One small village situated in the haute Languedoc has transformed its famous thermal springs into a worldwide brand of high quality skin care products. Avène, with its population of less than 500 people is home to the thermal spring of Saint Odile. The healing properties of the water were first discovered in 1736 by a Marquis as treatment for his horses' skin infection. By 1826, the site had been recognized in the medical literature as an effective treatment for a range of skin ailments. Such was its reputation that bottles of the water were sent to victims of the Chicago fire to help with burn treatments. Over the centuries the St Odile spring continued to offer treatments until in 1975, Pierre Fabre, a pharmacist from the area realized its broader potential and developed the expertise and products that today are recognized worldwide for their therapeutic benefits.

∞

Monique's recipe choices for May reflect the transition from spring to summer. The fresh peas, carrots, potatoes, broad beans, radishes, asparagus and onions are now showing up in the local markets so its time for a spring vegetable mélange. She has selected two other vegetable dishes that are tasty, work well hot or cold and are great buffet dishes. May is also the start of fresh lamb and Monique has a favourite recipe to share.

SPRING VEGETABLE MÉLANGE

The best part of this recipe is the trip to your favourite market to select whatever new vegetables are appearing. If possible, access local markets or visit local farms in your area.

Ingredients for 4 persons:

Sufficient quantities of whatever vegetables strike your fantasy. Remember that this may be such a hit that you will need more than you expect. Colour, shape, texture make for interesting combinations.

Salt and pepper to taste

Fresh thyme

The key to a successful mélange is to cook them until they are almost tender. The crunch and snap of freshly cooked vegetables will remind those gathered around the table of the pleasures of spring.

Preparation:

Prepare vegetables by peeling and slicing where needed-carrots, potatoes, onions, radishes. Trim ends of beans, asparagus; shell peas or leave whole depending on the variety.

In a large pot of salted water, drop in each group of vegetables separately. They will likely take a few minutes to reach the al dente stage. Remove the batch and plunge into ice water 30 seconds to stop the cooking process. Drain and set aside and continue with the rest of the vegetables. They can be prepared ahead of time

Just before serving, heat olive oil in a fry pan and add all the vegetables. Heat until vegetables are warmed through. Place in serving dish, add fresh thyme and salt and pepper.

TIAN AUX LÉGUMES

This is one of those French recipes that is so simple to make but looks great and tastes wonderful. Monique serves this for a light supper along with a cheese plate and fresh bread. Again, it works well hot or cold.

Ingredients for 4 persons:

3-4 tomatoes-the freshest and tastiest you can find

2-3 onions-sweet onions are best

2 medium zucchini

6 branches of fresh thyme, stripped of the leaves

1-2 tablespoons of olive oil

Salt and pepper to taste

1 package of chèvre to be cut in rounds
and placed over vegetables

Preparation:

Thinly slice the tomatoes, zucchini and onions in rounds

Oil a baking dish then beginning at one end, layer each item in rows, alternating colours-tomatoes, onions, zucchini, tomatoes, etc.

Sprinkle with thyme, salt & pepper and cover with sliced chèvre rounds

Bake at 350°F for approximately 30 minutes. This dish works well with a platter of cold meats and a chilled rosé wine.

NAVARIN D'AGNEAU

Monique describes this recipe as the harbinger of spring. It will likely be the last of the hearty stews of winter but provides the glimpse of the coming season of abundance. She recommends using *mange touts* peas that are known in North America as edible pea pods. If French mange touts are not available but fresh peas are ready, then after shelling the peas, Monique adds a few pea pods to the recipe for some extra flavour. She maintains that the secret is to use new spring vegetables to enhance the flavours. In France, the butcher tends to leave fat and bone on the cuts. That, I think, is what provides the rich taste to foods. I was amazed to watch Monique prepare this recipe when she simply sprinkled the flour over the vegetables and then added the water. I assumed that the result would be lumpy gravy. But nothing of the sort happened. Instead, the sauce was smooth, rich and tinged a lovely bronze colour that Monique said was due to the flour and fat combining.

Ingredients for 4 people:

2 pounds lamb shoulder cut into large chucks with fat attached

6-8 small onions

8-12 small carrots

8-12 small turnips

8-12 small potatoes

2 cloves garlic

24 green beans

24 pea pods or the peas from 24 pea pods, including 4 pea pods

2 tomatoes, cut into eighths

2 tablespoons flour

3 cups water

Salt and pepper to taste

Olive oil for sauteing

Preparation:

Liberally coat large pot with olive oil and add lamb pieces in small batches

Cook lamb until nicely browned on all sides. When finished, set aside.

Slowly add all remaining ingredients except potatoes to the pot and turn to coat on all sides. Allow to lightly brown in the fat.

Sprinkle the vegetables with flour, turn to coat them and then return the lamb chunks to the pot.

Add the water, cover pot and bring to a simmer. Allow the mixture to cook slowly until almost tender then add the potatoes. This dish is best prepared the day before serving to allow the flavours to mature. This dish worked well with a rosé from the local Cave Cooperative, fresh bread from the boulangerie and a salad of local greens.

JUNE

Historic festivals, picnics, 2CV,
coastal forts, Catalonia

June is the start of the main tourist season in Languedoc although the huge crowds have yet to appear. It is an ideal time to get a head start on the highlights of the region. Local artisans have been working hard all winter and spring to produce high quality pottery and art; international, national, regional and local festivals are all happening this month; there is a coastline of forts, abbeys and castles to visit and it's picnic time-time to grab fresh produce, cheeses, breads, meats and wine and head for the hills!

Pezenas is a town located in the heart of Languedoc that has made its reputation as a cultural centre based on the work of a young man who arrived here in 1647. Moliere and his troupe, Illustre Theatre, spent several years here entertaining the visiting royalty. Today, his name lives on in a ten-day festival in mid-June. Visitors are invited to walk in the footsteps of Moliere and to discover his works through a variety of venues held throughout the town. In addition to daily presentations on the significance and interpretation of Moliere's works, there are nightly performances of high quality theatre offering a wide choice of productions. There are costume parades, sporting events such as street sword fights, music festivals and street entertainment to make this the highlight of the Pezenas cultural season.

We joined the crowd, many of whom were dressed in period costume, as they moved through the old streets of Pezenas. Turning into Place Gambetta, we stepped back into time as the whole square had been decorated in seventeenth century style. We rushed back to the protection of the walls as horsemen galloped into the square, jumped off their horses and drew their swords. Men dressed as cavaliers held back the crowds as the swordsmen enacted a scene from long ago. The action ended as quickly as it had begun and the actors dispersed amid great applause. As we walked along the cobblestone street of old Pezenas, it was easy to picture life in the time of Moliere. The hotels he stayed in, the remnants of the old theatres, even the sedan chair positioned in the courtyard at the fifteenth century Hotel de LaCoste remain as reminders of his contribution to Pezenas life.

While Pezenas focuses on Moliere, numerous other towns and villages throughout the region organize similar thematic festivals. Carcassonne holds a music festival that features famous and budding musicians from all over the world. There is no end of cultural events to choose from throughout Languedoc. Information is available from any Office de Tourisme, local newspaper and magazines.

∞

France is covered in small, paved back roads that beckon one to explore the depths of the French countryside. June is the ideal time to head to the local market and choose from a wide variety of foods and wines to make up the perfect picnic basket. The Saturday markets in Pezenas, Carcassonne and Nîmes, the Sunday market in Narbonne or the weekly markets that spring up in all villages throughout Languedoc offer a chance to fulfill this most iconic of French country experiences.

> The Pezenas market runs several blocks down the Cour Jean Jaures with more than one hundred mechants setting their wares out on tables shaded by umbrellas and the large plane trees that line the south end of the Cour. I begin at the south end and do a first reconnoitering of all the fruit and vegetable stalls. Today, I am looking for vegetables that I will prepare

as *crudités* (raw vegetables) for our picnic. After checking over all the produce, I head towards the stall of M et Mme Arnaud. This elderly couple have sold their local produce for years and are well known as friendly but shrewd merchants. They *fait coucou* (beckon) me over to try a sample of fresh cherries. All of their products come from their farm or other local farmers. They sell only what is in season and grow only local varieties. I expect to see less than perfect supermarket produce but I know that it will taste wonderful. Today, he has fresh lettuce from his garden and after I point to the head I want, he takes it and carefully shakes off the excess dirty. I'm happy that I'm not paying by weight on this item. He then encourages me to sample some fresh peas and carrots and of course, they too end up in my *panier* (shopping basket). He carefully counts out the coins I hand him and politely hands me back my change. At this point, he offers me un petit cadeau of a bunch of small radishes. After our "bonne journees", I head over to other stalls to complete my purchases. I particularly enjoy the young Arab seller with his rapid-fire speech and frenzied manner. I select large bunches of fresh mint and fennel along with other vegetables and he quickly processes my purchases all the while calling out to his brothers on the other side. I momentarily feel transported to some souk in Morocco. At almost every stall, there will be samples of fruits and vegetables to taste. It is hard to resist the lure of the freshness and price.

I pass quickly through the long gauntlet of the clothes, shoes and fabric stalls as I make my way to the other end of the Cour where all the other food merchants are located. Again, samples are offered, merchants call out and beckon you to try their wares. As in all large markets, each vendor specializes in certain products: there are horse meat and beef butchers, then the pork sellers with their array of prepared specialty cold meats hanging from hooks, then the chicken and fowl stalls with their hanging birds and finally the large trays of prepared foods and the BBQ chicken rotisscric. Further along comes the fish stalls, cheese stalls, dried fruits and spice stalls, olives and other pickled delicacies stalls and finally, the bread stalls where gargantuan loaves are on view and you are asked to indicate how big a slice you want. After a dizzying experience of making my selections for the picnic, I needed a drink and headed for one of the local bars strategically situated along the Cour. Refreshed by a morning Pastis, I set out for home.

∞

To enjoy a true experience of a picnic in the French countryside, one should do it in the iconic French car-a Citroen 2CV. First designed and developed before WW11, the premise for the car was that a farmer could carry a pig to market and a crate of eggs over the ploughed fields without causing any damage to the pig or breaking any eggs. It had to be fixable with a screwdriver and pliers and must fit a tall man wearing a top hat. It first came into production after WW11 and sold successfully throughout the world until 1990. It is now a collector's car but still sees regular service in the villages, vineyards and back roads of France. Even on highways, it is given respect and allowed to motor along at its maximum speed of 100kms per hour, although it is happier bustling along at 60kms per hour. Thanks to some enterprising companies in Languedoc, it is now possible to rent a 2CV and relive this piece of French experience.

> Ever since my first trip to France, my dream was to drive a 2CV and tootle around the French countryside. When I saw the ad for "Cornelia Rent a Duck" I knew that my time had come. We picked up a car and along with the picnic basket stowed in the trunk, we headed out into the countryside. There is something magical about rolling back the canvas top, feeling the wind blow your hair and the sun beaming down. The 2CV is surprisingly comfortable given the obvious lack of twenty-first century engineering. The steering was nimble as we maneuvered the windiest roads we could find. Finally, we turned the corner and there before us was a perfect picnic site. We pulled off the road and bumped along the grassy verge, stopping under the shade of a large chestnut tree. We looked out over the

Orb Valley straight down to the sea. The steep sides of the valley were covered with diagonal rows of vines, soaking up the warm summer sun. The air was still and the hawks soared above us. We could see an old stone house tucked into a ravine down near the valley floor but otherwise, we felt the solitude of the quiet Languedoc back country.

Out from the trunk came our folding table and chairs, tablecloth, plates and glasses as we laid out a proper French picnic. However, we discovered that had we forgotten to bring chairs, we could have simply popped out the back seat and used it instead.

We sipped on a cool aperitif of *peche sauvage* (wild peach) accompanied by local Lucque olives and almonds. Next came the crudités, paté and cold meats, fresh baquette and a rosé from the region. Our entrée was sardines from Collioure drizzled with local olive oil and lemon. The plat was cold chicken from the market rotisserie accompanied by Monique's recipe for green beans and potato salad. The pace was slow and the only interruption was the cyclist who slowed as he passed, calling out "bonne appetit". The cheese course included a fresh chèvre from Mas Rolland and a blue cheese from the Larzac causse. Finally, fresh cherries and a pine nut tarte from the boulangerie finished the meal and almost finished us.

Andrea Swan with Monique Guezel

Helas, (too bad), the only responsible thing to do was to lie down in the warm sun and take advantage of the quiet afternoon. We meandered home enjoying the looks and friendly honks we received from other motorists. "Matilde" as I named the car, was a delight to drive and has added immensely to my memories of time in France.

For the 2CV enthusiast, there are several local clubs that offer the chance to work on cars or purchase vintage Citroens. In the village of Montblanc, a group of eager enthusiasts spend hours rebuilding and repairing classic Citroen cars. Their collection of 2CVs, DSs with the stunningly inventive hydraulic system and the classic Traction Avants featured in so many old movies is a treat to visit. The fellows are easy to talk to and patient with French novices. They sell their cars and compared to North American prices, they are a bargain.

∞

As a country with three coastlines, France has always been a seafaring nation but it has also meant that she was exposed to invasions from the sea. During the twelfth and thirteenth centuries, this weakness led to the development of a series of fortifications along the seacoast. Today, there are several that remain and they offer wonderful opportunities for exploration. The two best preserved are at Aigue-Morts on the eastern side of the region, close to the Rhone river and Le Forteresse de Salses on the western side close to the Spanish border.

Aigues Mortes has been inhabited from 100 BC by the Romans. Over time, the early remnants of previous civilizations have been replaced by the massive fortified town constructed during the reign of Louis IX. Built on salt marshes, the ramparts rise majestically out of the flatness of the surrounding countryside. Inside, a complete town exists although today, it is overrun not by enemies but by tourists who come to experience what life might have been like centuries ago. Over the centuries, the land and sea surrounding Aigues Mortes have provided a home to prehistoric dwellers, retired Roman sailors, the Crusaders in the twelfth century as they prepared for the Crusades in the Holy Land, the Knights Templar who were incarcerated here in the fourteenth century, the Huguenots who were given refuge in the seventeenth century and the salt merchants who mined the valuable marshes in the nineteenth century. Laid out in a square pattern, Aigues Mortes represents rivals Carcassonne as a fortified city. Both reflect the building techniques of their ears and the use of defensive walls and streets to hinder the enemy. The walls and interior buildings of Aigues Mortes have remained intact and offer an excellent example of medieval and renaissance architecture.

On the other end of Languedoc where the Pyrenees run down to the Mediterranean lies the Forteresse de Salses, a fifteenth century complex that in its time stood guard over the Spanish province of Catalonia and ensured that the French enemy could not easily pass along the coastal route into Spain. It was in 1642 that France won the area of Catalonia that now makes up the Pyrenées Orientale. The Forteresse was not as big as Aigues Mortes but remains a well-preserved example of Spanish architecture of the period. A fundamental difference between Aigues Mortes and the Forteresse is that Salses was built on a mineral spring, ensuring that the population had a secure source of water while Aigues Mortes relied on dug wells or water being carted in. Lack of water was often the reason that besieged populations succumbed to defeat. The enemy simply waited them out until thirst and starvation forced the population into submission.

Over the centuries, the struggle for control of lands between France and Spain resulted in numerous campaigns to build and re-build fortifications all along the frontiers. For any history buff, there is an opportunity to visit these remains while at the same time, exploring the diversity of the Catalan culture that has flourished here regardless of rulers. It is possible to do a circle tour beginning in Salses and heading up into the high Pyrenées.

From Salses, the exploration of forts, abbeys and fortified villages continues along the western coastline to Perpignan and Collioure. Then, moving inland from the coastline, Amelie les Bains is the first of the fortified hilltop towns. From there, one climbs to Fort Lagarde, overlooking the small town of Prats de Mollo.

If you are in need of some retail therapy, a short detour off the road from Prats de Mollo will lead you to Saint Laurent de Cerdans and into the heart of the Catalan weaving industry. Here, you will find the "Sunshine fabrics" that have been woven since 1873 and make up the colourful striped fabric seen throughout Languedoc. The weavers have created a line of table linens, deck chair fabric and that well-known Catalan favourite, espadrilles. Here, these canvas and rope shoes are known as "Vigatanes" and were especially designed to be able to dance the Catalonian "Sardane".

From here the journey leads across the border into Spain as there is no direct highway route around "Canigou," the highest point in the Pyrenées. Instead, one travels towards Ripoll and Puigcerda before returning back to France to pick up the trail of the fortified villages. If you've had enough history for the moment, nearby Andorra, with its duty free shopping, might be a quick refreshing break. Otherwise, the route continues to Villefranche de Conflent, a small village nestled high up in the Pyrenées between the confines of the river Tet and river Cady. The whole town lies within fortified walls last reconstructed under the supervision of the famous French Marshall, Vauban. Further up the valley lies the Fort Mont Louis. This well pre-served bastion is the property of the French army but visitors are welcome to walk around parts of it.

For the not faint of heart, the *Train Jaune* (Ligne de Certagne) offers an exciting chance to travel between Villefranche and Mont Louis on a narrow gauge train. Travelling thirty nine miles up to an altitude of fifty-two hundred feet, the train passes over two bridges and through nineteen tunnels. For the thrill-seekers, there are open cars that provide breath-taking views of the deep chasms and winding tracks.

The last stop on the journey offers the chance to recover from the history overload and the hair-raising ride up to Mont Louis. St. Martin de Canigou has perched on the side of Canigou since 1009. Today, this abbey that can only be accessed by a thirty-minute walk from the town of Caseil, is home to the Community of the Beatitudes. This religious community offers visitors hospitality and spiritual retreat from a busy world.

Overall, this tour of French Catalonia provides a glimpse of a vibrant and colourful region known for its proud, independent spirit, wonderful striped textiles and a cuisine that more closely resembles that of the Basque country with an emphasis on fresh, colourful foods, simply prepared.

∞

Monique has picked up the Catalan theme in selecting June's recipes by focusing on fresh, colourful produce and local seafood. Zucchini, tomatoes and local onions from Perpignan are now appearing in the markets.

LEGUMES FARCIS (STUFFED)

Monique described this recipe as a basic one-meal dish that works well either hot or cold. As we discussed what else might be served with this dish, Monique explained that one would start with an *entrée*, followed by this *plat*. In France, unlike America, the word, entrée, on the menu means starter. Plat is the main dish.

As Monique and I prepare and cook each dish, the routine is that I watch her and then rapidly write down what she is doing and convert her actions into measurements and instructions. When she grabs some salt, I have to figure out what the amount is so that I can include it in the recipe. As we prepared this dish, I was trying to determine how much bread was in her hand. She informed me that "le bonne chef ne measure pas" the good cook doesn't measure anything but senses what is needed and tastes the mixture to correct the seasonings. The recipes in this book have been translated from Monique's actions and then tested for taste and consistency against Monique's results. I explained that most North American cooks rely on recipes rather than "le bonne chef". Perhaps, one has to cook in France to feel comfortable being "un bonne chef."

Ingredients for 4 persons:

2 pounds minced veal and pork-half and half

1 cup day old bread torn apart in small pieces

1 clove garlic-finely minced

2 eggs

Fresh chopped parsley

Salt and pepper to taste

4 tomatoes

2 onions

2 small eggplants

4 round small zucchini

Safflower or canola oil to drizzle on vegetables

Preparation:

Wash all the vegetables.

Cut off the bottom of each tomato and set aside, leaving the stem end intact, scoop out the seeds and centers and discard. By cutting off the bottom rather than the top, the tomato will sit in the pan without rolling around.

Cut eggplants lengthwise and cut off ends. Carefully scoop out centers trying to keep the piece intact. Set aside.

Cut off the tops of zucchini and set aside. Carefully scoop out the seeds of the zucchini. If using long zucchini, cut lengthwise and scoop out centers.

Cut onions in half across widest part and scoop out centers. Set aside.

Moisten bread in small amount of water to permit tearing. Discard any excess water.

Mix together meat, bread, eggs, garlic.

Add salt and pepper-Monique cranked the pepper mill about 10 times and the salt mill about 14 times

Add chopped parsley and mix well with stuffing.

Divide the mixture evenly into each vegetable, pressing lightly into the craters of the vegetable.

Place each vegetable together in a large baking dish.

Cover the tomatoes and the zucchini with their *chapeaux* (the cut off tops) and cut up any remaining onion or eggplant into the dish for added flavour.

Drizzle the oil over the vegetables until each one has a small amount of oil on them.

Sprinkle a bit of water in base of the pan.

Bake in 350°F oven for approximately 90 minutes until top is bubbly and golden. May be served hot or cold with bread, green salad and a crisp wine.

PIPERADE

We were introduced to this dish in a tiny village in the foothills of the western Pyrenées. It is a classic Basque dish made up of the local ingredients, such as onions, tomatoes and green peppers. The server pointed out to us that the red, white and green colours of the piperade represent the colours of the Basque flag. Monique described how these recipes spread throughout Languedoc with the arrival of Spanish immigrants or the seasonal workers who travel through Languedoc to find work during the grape harvest. For me, it was another example of how Languedoc has, over the centuries, been such an incubator of new foods, arts and culture.

Ingredients for 6 persons:

1 coarsely diced onion

3 green peppers, coarsely diced

2-3 tomatoes

$\frac{1}{4}$ cup olive oil

Salt and pepper to taste

Espelette pepper-this can often be found
in specialty stores in North America.

Herbs de Provence-which is made up of thyme,
oregano, rosemary, savory and marjoram

Preparation:

In large skillet, add olive oil, diced onion and place on medium heat. Cook gently until lightly golden.

Add the peppers and stir. Cover pan and reduce heat.

Here is the interesting part-as I watched Monique prepare the tomatoes, she was using the back of a knife and slowly, with some force, bringing it down over the tomato in rows starting from the stem to the bottom. I asked her what she was doing and she said, "je le caresse" ("I am caressing the tomato.") This was such an intriguing response as I had never heard this cooking term before. She explained that rather than blanching the tomatoes to remove the skin, "caressing" them is much quicker and works just as well. She then proceeded to remove the stem end and easily peeled back the skin in strips. She then cut the tomato in half, removed the seeds and diced the flesh into the onion, and pepper mix once the peppers were soft.

Add salt and pepper and herbes de Provence or espelette pepper. For a true Basque piperade, use the mild espelette pepper or for Monique's version, use herbe de Provence. Both add excellent flavour to the dish. Cover and let simmer for *une bonne heure* (a long time over low heat). In this case, we left it for almost 90 minutes. The mixture will be almost mushy with a wonderful smell. It is delicious served hot or cold, by itself or over scrambled eggs.

VELOUTÉ DE
PETIT POIS

Spring peas are now appearing in the markets and this is one of Monique's soups that she prepares for the evening meal during June. It is delicious served cold as an entrée for 4 persons for lunch or heated and served with fresh bread for supper for 2 persons.

Ingredients for 4 persons:

3 cups of freshly shelled peas. You can use the same amount of frozen peas with similar results

1 tablespoon butter

1 cup chopped leeks, may include some of the green part

1 chopped medium onion

½ cup tightly packed fresh mint leaves

Salt & pepper

3 cups of chicken broth or water
with a chicken bouillon cube

Chopped chives

3-4 tablespoons crème fraiche

Preparation:

Sauté the onions and leeks until soft and tender

Add the peas in the butter for 3-5 minutes depending on whether you are using frozen or fresh peas (fresh peas will take longer to cook)

Bring the chicken broth to a soft boil. Add onions, peas, mint, salt and pepper

Purée mixture until smooth (it may be necessary to purée in small batches to achieve a smooth soup)

Soup may be chilled at this point.

Garnish with chopped chives and crème fraiche.

GAZPACHO

Catalan foods are present in many excellent recipes but they are also appearing in many prepared products available at the local supermarkets. Gazpacho is one such product. This tomato-based vegetable soup is traditionally served cold, garnished with croutons and crème fraiche. In France, in the refrigerator section of most stores, you can find fresh gazpacho made by Avalle and packaged in what looks like a milk carton. I don't know how they do it but they have managed to capture such freshness. They make a number of soups but this one is our favourite for a hot summer day.

JULY

*travelling with children, Bastille Day, tour
de France, summer drinks, festivals*

The heat of summer is here and the *sud de France* (south
of France) lives up to its reputation as a place that thrives on
great food and wine, a vast array of activities and a tourists'
mecca. July is an ideal time to visit if you are a sun worshiper
but want to avoid the crowds. The beach resorts are welcoming,
the villages are coming alive in their attempts to draw people in,
the locals are basking in the sunshine and demonstrating that
quintessential Southern French art of *flanerie* (strolling along).
This is the month when grape growers can rest and allow the
sun to do its magic, not only on grapes but also on aching
muscles and bones. There is a general sense in the villages that

this is the month of repose; the work in the vines is done for now and attention can be paid to family and friends. July is also the month of two great events-Bastille Day on July 14th and the 23 day Tour de France that is almost guaranteed to pass through Languedoc at some stage of the tour. And for music lovers, July is the chance to immerse oneself in great jazz, folk and world music as Sete, Mèze, Montpellier, and Carcassonne all host festivals throughout the month. July is an especially great time to visit with children. The French school year is longer than most North American school years with summer holidays usually beginning the second week of July and other European countries even later in July. This means that families have not yet begun to travel so while most resorts and tourist areas are open, the crowds have yet to appear. In many cases, the high season rates have not started so vacation costs for families are reduced. In addition to the myriad of activities available in the seaside villages, there are some inland activities that would provide wonderful holiday memories for young people.

∞

For any budding paleontologist, finding dinosaur bones and fragments are a dream come true. Given the diversity of pre-historic remains in Languedoc, it is an ideal place to explore. One of the best examples of dinosaur remains is at the Dinosaur Park near Mèze. For young children, there is an outdoor walking tour featuring numerous full-scale models of well-known species. There is even a chance to dig for egg fragments in the sand pits. An interpretative centre, picnic area and café make this a popular destination point after sunny days at the beach.

Alain and Christophe, the two busy, seven year old sons of our neighbours, are keen dinosaur hunters and love to share their enthusiasm. We set off one Wednesday afternoon to explore the Dinosaur Park, not sure what to expect and how these little boys might react. Off we went and as we approached the park, the large tyrannosauras rex loomed near the entrance. The chatty comments in the back seat stopped immediately and a hushed silence settled in the car as we moved forward to the ticket booth. Inside the park, as we walked along the trails, we came upon all the dinosaurs that had so captured our young friends' imagination. There were troglodons about to pounce, a huge triceratops protecting its young from a T-rex and a stegosauraus spreading its spines in a defensive position. We were sure that the bulging eyes of our young charges would never resolve as they cautiously approached each animal, uncertain if it was real or not. Were those huge teeth and vicious claws about to turn on them? By the time we arrived at the sand pit, they were assured that all was well and were ready to begin their hunt for dinosaur eggs. The day ended with a visit to the well-stocked gift shop and an animated ride home for two tired but happy little boys.

Still within Languedoc, one can visit the site of pre-historic man and see evidence of life 450,000 years ago. Tauteval is located in the Pyrenees-Orientales and is an easy drive from anywhere in Languedoc. The interpretation centre is very interactive and provides excellent cultural and recreational activities.

∞

Journeying from pre-historic to ancient civilizations, the centre of Narbonne is a network of subterranean tunnels and passageways that are the remains of the former Roman Horreum, the underground warehouse dating from the first century. Today, a sound and light show recreates the atmosphere of an ancient market day experience.

Our young visitors were enthusiastic to explore the Roman remains in Narbonne and after walking along the remains Roman Via Domitia, we proceeded to the Horreum located in behind the cathedral. Down we went into the labyrinth and as we did, the sense of being transported back in time overtook us. As we passed a large storage vaults, the clopping of horses feet behind us made us jump and seek safety behind a large Roman pillar. Of course, there was nothing there but the realistic effect made us look. We knew that we were the only people in the tunnels yet voices called out from all around, accents and words we could not understand. The woman who sold us the tickets had asked if we wanted her to accompany us and now we knew why. The children were frightened as we moved deeper into the passageways and although it was not dark, the eeriness of the place was disconcerting and we longed for the reality of the twenty-first century. As we hurried through the tunnels, concerned about taking a wrong turn, we kept seeing remnants of long ago vestiges of market life. It was a pleasure to burst out into the July sunshine into the rush of the busy Sunday morning Narbonne market and realize that the sounds that we had just heard in the Horreum were the same sounds we were now hearing all around us as buyers and sellers continued the centuries old practices of the marketplace.

∞

If animals are of greater interest for young visitors, then the Reserve Africaine at Sigean, the Montpellier Zoo or the Seaquarium at Grau de Roi are all worth a visit. As one drives through the park, the Reserve Afraicaine has more than 3800 animals and birds living in natural surroundings. It is a chance to see lions, bears, giraffes and zebras along with a host of other animals lazing about watching the funny people in cars drive slowly by. There are walking areas that bring you close to elephants, chimpanzees, snakes, alligators and turtles but otherwise the visitors view the animals from the safety of their car.

The Montpellier Zoo is home to a broad range of animals, birds, reptiles and fish. Located in the north end of the city, the zoo provides a great day trip for young visitors as a break from the seaside resorts of La Grande Motte and Palavas les Flots. If staying closer to the seaside resorts works best, then the Seaquarium at Grau du Roi may fill the bill for young enthusiasts. With its series of pools and connecting trails, it is easy to move from the seals and sea lions to sharks, turtles and tropical fish with over 200 species in all. Of particular interest may be the Requinarium, an area dedicated to the study and protection of sharks and the only one of its kind in Europe. While these are the biggest attraction of their kind, there are smaller venues dedicated to wolves, bison and Australian animals located throughout Languedoc. Needless to say, there is something to satisfy any child young or old alike.

∞

While not unique to Languedoc, swimming parks can make for a welcome break from museum visits for active young visitors. Some of the biggest are along the coast at Aqualand at Cap d'Agde, Espace Grande Bleue at La Grande Motte near Montpellier and the swimming pool at Sete. They all offer great water slides and multiple pools. As well, most towns and large villages have pools and offer tickets for visitors. One note of caution in French public pools: bathing caps are mandatory and swim suits must meet specific criteria. This means that for males, speedos are the acceptable wear and for girls, sports wear-type bathing suits will likely not be allowed but a two piece or speedo style suit would be acceptable. There are no such restrictions on beaches in France and the only issue may be the prevalence of topless sunbathers.

∞

For some travelers, their children are the four-legged kind. France is a country that welcomes people travelling with cats and dogs. It is not unusual to see small dogs sitting quietly next to its owner on a chair in a restaurant. Large dogs lie contentedly under bar stools or tables awaiting the master. Dogs wander hopefully through the markets and are often rewarded with scrapes of meat or fish. Interestingly, it is rare to see fights or signs of aggression. The down side of all this doggy freedom is that it is always a good idea to walk the streets gazing at the sidewalk as there are few laws regarding picking up after dogs. This is slowly changing and is becoming less of an issue but be prepared.

Bringing a pet to France is easy. Airline charges and rules for having a small animal in the cabin are reasonable. Health regulations require documentation for rabies and general good health. There is no quarantine period. Hotels accept small pets although B&B or private accommodations may have restrictions. Pet food brands are often the same as North America. Veterinary clinics are common in all towns and villages and the staff often speak some English. They are of excellent quality with very reasonable pricing.

> We decided after much consideration to bring our elderly cat with us to France. Our local vet assured us that this was a wise decision and that Brutus would travel well in the cabin with us without any sedation. After a few successful trial runs in the car, we made final preparations with the understanding that he might end up with my niece in Toronto if the first leg of the flight was a disaster. He was incredible with not a peep out of him during the five hour flight. The total transit time including the four hour train ride was fifteen hours and he slept most of the time. When we arrived at the house, he ambled out of his small carry case, smelled around and settled

into his new home. As the vet had predicted, he was happiest with us regardless of where we were living. He quickly made friends with the little female garden cat and became more active and curious. He adapted well after only a few days and I'm not sure, but even his "meow" seemed to have a French accent to it! Our return home was equally uneventful and within minutes of arrival, he had checked out his old haunt and settled in.

So if anyone feels that they cannot travel to France because of their pets, rest assured that there are many options to ensure a successful adventure.

∞

Between 1789 and 1799, the French revolted against the monarchy and the Church to break down the hierarchical society and establish one rooted in the motto "Liberté, Eqalitié, Fraternité". The customs, rules and institutions present in France today bear witness to the fight carried out more than two hundred years ago. The storming of the Bastille, the Paris prison, on July 14th, 1790 is a major celebration against the tyranny of the time. Every hamlet, village and town throughout France will mark this day with fireworks, parties and organized events that visitors can participate in.

No sooner had we arrived in the village for the start of our holiday, than Serge came knocking at our front door inviting us to the street party that was organized for July 14th. Promptly at noon, we headed down the street to the narrow alleyway below us. It had been cordoned off to traffic and tables lined the alleyway from end to end.

As visitors, we were shown to a place of honour in the middle of the dining tables and then brought over to the aperitif table. Laden with hors d'oeurves, alcohol of all descriptions and goodies for the children, the tables were surrounded by the locals. Of course, we had to begin the party with a Pastis, the licorice flavoured alcoholic drink characteristic of the south of France. Serge poured us a generous helping, "two fingers-the thumb and the little finger". We watched as others quickly swallowed their drinks and then slowly sipped ours, knowing that the heat of the noon sun and our empty stomachs made us ready targets for an unsteady gait if we followed their example and swigged down the beverage. Our plates were heaped with food to soak up the liquor and after standing around chatting to friends and neighbours, we were encouraged to move to the tables. Sitting across from us was M et Mme Ortez from up the street. M Ortez had clearly begun drinking much earlier than the rest of us and Mme was chastising him in rapid French. When she realized who we were, she immediately broke from her rant to share a story with us. Months before, our son had been staying at the house and was baking a cake. Early one morning, he arrived at her door in search of a cup of sugar. She was so enchanted by this tall young man who could speak French and could cook that she just had to share the news with us. By the time she was finished, M Ortez had made his escape. The meal was set to begin. In front of each person was a heaping plate of freshly steamed mussels from Sete. Having no idea what was to follow, we tucked in with enthusiasm and soon our plates were empty. The breadbaskets were passed along and frequently refilled in order to soak up the delicious white wine sauce from the mussels. Of course, along with the plates came bottles of local white wines. This first course of mussels was followed by a palate cleanser—half a fresh melon filled with porto. We assumed this was dessert then as the plates were whisked away by the local teenagers, we noticed that three men had arrived carrying a massive, flat-bottomed pan on their shoulders. Unsure of what was happening, we pointed and asked Mme Ortez. "Hoopla, c'est la paella" she exclaimed. Before we knew it, a large plate of rice, prawns, chicken and mussels was sitting before each of us. As we quietly loosened our belts and tucked in, we wondered how we were ever going to get through this. Slowly but surely, the plates of paella disappeared. I did notice that several local dogs were quietly threading through the chairs and legs under the table. I am

Andrea Swan with Monique Guezel

sure that their efforts did not go unrewarded. By this time, it was two-thirty and some of us were beginning to flag. Undaunted, the organizing committee passed out more wine and then the requisite cheese course. Each person received a small round of brie. As we protested that we could not eat another thing, they graciously allowed us to share a cheese round. At this point, people were engaged in quiet conversation with tablemates. It was an ideal chance to be included in the life of our quartier. After a significant period, the dessert tray was brought out and tarte tatin slices were placed in front of each person. Somehow, we managed to find a small place to hide away this tasty treat. By the end of the meal, we were surprised to find that although we had eaten much more than normal and did feel full, we did not feel over-stuffed and once the music started, we were quite able to join the long line of people snaking in and out of the tables. We headed home around five thirty to the music going strong and young and old alike dancing away the calories. We have subsequently heard stories from visitors that they have participated in these events all over the region. We certainly felt that we participated in the July 14th celebrations and had been part of the freedom, equality and brotherhood of our neighbourhood. The only event yet to come was the fireworks display that evening. It gave us another chance to engage with locals as they celebrated this annual recognition of the hard fought values of their country.

∞

The Tour de France is a highlight of July in Languedoc since its inception in 1903 Almost without exception, it passes through Languedoc enroute to the two major mountain areas of the Pyreneés and the Alps, making it possible to catch a glimpse of the whirl of riders as they streak past.

> We were excited when we realized that the Tour de France route was coming through our village. We watched the evening news with great anticipation as each day they provided details on the teams threading their way towards us, ending stage after stage with someone else sporting the yellow leader's jersey. We watched on TV as they crawled up the grueling mountain passes only to hurl down the other side in the closely packed formation. Today was the day they would come through the village. We secured our spots along the side of the narrow road on the edge of town, wondering how close we should sit to escape being swept up as they raced past. Here we were at one of the major sporting events and we didn't have to pay for a ringside seat. The race is so carefully timed that we knew within a half hour when they would be passing. Not wanting to miss anything, we arrived in plenty of time and set up our chairs. As the time approached, we could see

more and more vans passing along the roadway followed by helicopters bearing famous television logos. The vehicle cluster increased so we knew that the moment had come. Suddenly, the police motorcycle escort appeared, closely followed by a blur. That was it! The first peloton had passed as a blurred mass of colour with absolutely no chance to identify any individual cyclists. Once we overcame our surprise at the rapidity of the event, we waited for the slower cyclists and marveled at their grace and athleticism as they sped by. Again, a fleet of vans passed, many with bicycles strapped to the top or large red crosses on them signaling emergency vehicles. We watched the stage on TV that evening and realized that while it provided a better view of the individual riders, it gave nothing of the thrill of being there in person.

∞

Strung along the coastline like beads of a necklace, lies several coastal towns such as Agde, Sete, Port la Nouvelle and Leucate. Originally islands surrounded by marshlands, these towns are now linked by sandy beaches creating inland lagoons. The lagoon linking Sete and Agde, Etang de Thau, is the largest of several along the coast. The lagoons along this portion of the Mediterranean coast are connected to the sea by underground tunnels allowing an exchange of fresh water and seawater. The Etang de Thau, because of its depth and size is home to a major oyster industry. Many of the small villages that skirt the seaside of the lagoon have active fishing fleets and offer cruises and tours of the area. Besides being home to a robust seafood industry, Sete is the site of several memorable festivals. Starting in late June, Sete is transformed into a major party town with international music performers who play well into the early hours. During a soccer world cup year, the festival adopts the themes of the host country making for an even livelier event.

For a somewhat more subdued musical experience, just down the road in Agde, the Fete de la Musique offers a somewhat more sedate atmosphere with a broad range of music and choral performances ranging from medieval and folk to modern jazz.

Port la Nouvelle and Leucate are much newer and offer a wealth of all-inclusive vacation accommodations. Leucate is home to international wind-surfing competitions.

∞

Now that summer is in full swing, you may find yourself invited to a *l'heure de l'apero* (happy hour) for an aperitif. The invitation is usually for the late afternoon or early evening as a way to stimulate the appetite before dinner. It is a chance for friends and neighbours to get together before returning to their own homes for dinner. It is not typically an invitation for the full evening. Champagne, rosé or aperitifs such as kir, Dubonnet, Lillet, Ricard, would be the common alcoholic beverages in Languedoc. *Une sirop with l'eau gazeause* (flavoured syrup with sparkling water) or lemonade would be offered as non-alcoholic beverages. Lemonade in France is often water and fresh lemon juice with a sugar bowl on the side for you to sweeten your own drink. Rather than the large assortment of hors d'ouvres that might be common at North American cocktail parties, nibblies such as nuts, olives, little sausages or chips may be the foods available.

The temperatures are now climbing quickly and by mid-day Monique has prepared meals for both the mid-day meal and supper. Her selections for July focus on easy to put together menus that can be prepared early in the morning. As she says, when the sun is hot, the foods should be cool and not too heavy.

AIOLI WITH CRUDITÉS

Aioli is a quintessential Mediterranean condiment that is used on a wide variety of vegetables, fish and meats. Basically, it's a garlic, mustard mayonnaise. I have been known to cheat and add minced garlic and mustard to a good store bought mayonnaise but when I suggested that to Monique, she quickly said that this is not how to prepare a vrai aioli. After trying Monique's aioli, I had to agree that there was no real comparison. Her aioli had so much more flavour and was a bright yellow colour.

As I laid out the ingredients for the aioli, Monique drew my attention to the eggs. On every store bought egg in France there is a faint red code on the shell of each egg. This code is a series of letters and numbers: 0 is organic, 1 is farmyard raised, the next number is the farm code and then the date it was laid. Monique says, eggs that are too fresh should not be used because the whites will be tough and the yolks will break easily. Monique does not refrigerate her eggs but keeps them in a basket in a cool part of her kitchen. Nor does she wash them before using them because she says that it removes the special coating that protects the eggs. The eggs I had bought at the local market came in a variety of sizes with some being bigger than any North American Extra Large eggs. For any of the recipes, I have used the equivalent of a large egg in North American standards.

Ingredients:

> 1 large egg yolk

> ½ clove of crushed garlic-Monique used a rosé garlic which has a fairly strong taste so you may need to adapt to garlic varieties available to you. The aioli should have a "nip" to it.

> 1 teaspoon Dijon mustard

> 3/4 cup extra virgin olive oil

> Salt & pepper

> 1 tablespoon fresh lemon juice

Preparation:

Crush the garlic and mix in salt & pepper.

Whisk together the egg yolk, crushed garlic mix, lemon juice and mustard.

Slowly (drop by drop) add the olive oil to the mixture, whisking continually and making sure that the oil is well mixed in before adding more. As the mixture thickens, you can add the oil more quickly.

Adjust the seasonings as needed

Refrigerate up to two days

You can also prepare this with a blender but Monique prefers to make aioli by hand. It's quick and easy and there is no blender to then have to clean. The secret is to add the olive oil slowing and blend well between additions.

Monique also indicated that you could substitute the garlic for other flavours such as curry but it would not be a vrai aioli.

Crudités

Crudités are a selection of fresh vegetables used for dipping in aioli. You are bound only by your imagination and the selection available at the local market. My assortment changes every time and the only constant is the wonderful strong flavour of the aioli. It makes a colourful addition to a summer meal with an accompanying plate of cold meats, bread and a chilled rosé.

As we prepared the plate, Monique talked about her other favourite uses for aioli. Cabillaud is a lovely, dense fish found in the markets. Monique fries it lightly and serves it with a light cover of aioli. Cabillaud is cod and readily available in the supermarket in the frozen food section in North America.

Soupe des Poisson

While hot, pureed fish soup does not seem like a typical summer dish, Monique said that it is a favourite that she serves often for a light supper. The secret ingredient is a dash of aioli added at the last minute to each bowl. When I asked how difficult it was to make, she laughed and said that this was one of her short cut meals. There is a brand at the market that she does not feel that she can prepare better herself so even the best cooks sometimes admit defeat.

Bouillabaisse

Our discussion on fish soups quickly led to the famous fish soup of the Mediterranean region, Bouillabaisse. Marseille claims ownership of the true recipe as it was originally a fish stew made by fishermen's wives from unsold fish in the famous Marseille market. Like so many of the traditional recipes, there are often a few key ingredients and then everything else is up to the cook. With bouillabaisse, there must be pieces of white fish, rockfish, clams and mussels. The stew is prepared by adding the fish piece by piece to a simmering broth containing carrots, leeks, onions, tomatoes, celery and potatoes. The other traditional addition is *rouille*, which is aioli with saffron and cayenne pepper added for colour and heat. Along the coast, restaurants typically serve the bouillabaisse as a single dish but *un vrai* bouillabaisse, according to Monique, will be served first with the broth, rouille and bread in a bowl and then the fish pieces presented as a second dish.

Because Monique did not grow up on the coast, it is not a part of her cooking tradition and therefore, she prefers to enjoy bouillabaisse in seaside restaurants where the ambiance and smell of the sea is part of the enjoyment.

SALAD NIÇOISE

Monique explained that although Nice may lay claim to the origins of this salad, it is common throughout Languedoc as an easy to prepare, light, summer salad. In a country that prides itself on the quality of its meat and fish products, it can be difficult for a vegetarian to find a variety of menu items. Monique substitutes garbanzo beans for the tuna et voilà, a perfect vegetarian meal.

Ingredients for 4:

4 hard boiled eggs

Green beans for 4

1 Sweet or red onion

1 can chunk tuna or broiled or smoked tuna

2 tomatoes or cherry tomatoes for 4

Black olives-niçoise olives are small and salty and may be available at specialty stores

2-3 Anchovies or sardines per person

2-3 potatoes

1 garlic clove

Mustard Vinaigrette

Of course, you can add other vegetables as you want-that is the beauty of these summer salads.

Preparation:

Parboil the potatoes until fork tender and then cube in large chunks

Blanche the green beans until tender

Split the garlic clove and remove the small centerpiece. Rub the serving plate well with the halves and discard

Arrange all the ingredients together on a large plate shortly before serving and drizzle with the vinaigrette

Mustard Vinaigrette

$^3/_4$ cup good olive oil

1 clove garlic

1 tbsp Dijon mustard

$^1/_4$ cup white wine vinegar

Salt & Pepper to taste

Cut the garlic clove in half to reveal the center and remove the small, green center from the clove, then mince the pieces. Monique explained that the small center of the garlic clove should always be removed before using the clove as the center will otherwise give indigestion.

Whisk together the vinegar, garlic and mustard until blended.

Slowly drizzle in the olive oil, continuing to whisk together

Add salt and pepper to taste.

Let sit for at least 30 minutes so that flavours can blend.

SARDINES IN LEMON

We tasted this simple dish during a visit to Collioure, the small, seaside town nestled between the foothills of the Pyrenées and the Mediterranean. The fresh sardines had been marinated in a mixture of lemon juice and olive oil. They were served with pieces of toast as an entrée. When I mentioned our experience to Monique, she explained that Collioure had a long tradition of preparing seafood and that salted anchovies or sardines can still be purchased from one of the two remaining businesses in Collioure-either le Famille Roque or Famille Desclaux. In testing this recipe back in North America, I could not find fresh sardines or anchovies so used a can of water–packed sardines. While I was unable to provide the backdrop of the blue sky and the turrets of the Templar castle, my guests did comment that the presentation and the taste reminded them of holidays in Languedoc.

Ingredients for 4 persons:

> 2 cans sardines packed in water if fresh sardines or anchovies are not available
>
> Juice of 2 lemons
>
> Finely sliced lemon for garnish
>
> Juice of 1 lime
>
> 1 finely sliced sweet onion
>
> 1 bay leave

Herbes de Provence

6-8 tablespoons olive oil

Pinch of cayenne pepper or espelette

Salt and pepper to taste

Preparation:

If using fresh fish, marinate them at least 12 hours before serving as the lemon juice "cooks" the fish

Gently remove the head (if present) and inner cord from each fish before marinating

Mix together all the ingredients except the fish and onions

Lay the fish in a shallow dish and cover with the marinade for at least 30 minutes. Refrigerate until ready to serve

Decorate the plate with the lemon and onion slices

Serve with small pieces of toasted bread.

AUGUST

patience, festivals, transportation routes,
beach life, mountain holidays, camping

August in Languedoc means a dramatic increase in tourists, especially French tourists, traffic slow downs, transportation unions *en greve* (strikes), heat, family time, festivals, every activity imaginable, and a carnival atmosphere. This is the month to truly experience the laid back, southern French lifestyle, to live the holiday season as the French do. One has to remember however, that the French have years of experience practising the August holiday routine. If needing to develop patience or practise the middle finger salute is on your "to do" list, then this is the ideal time to visit.

∞

Since 1929, France has had a system of paid vacation days for all unionized employees. The number of days has increased over the decades and is now officially set at five weeks of paid vacation time per year for all salaried employees, typically taken in late July or August. While the number of weeks of paid vacation may seem extraordinary by American standards, it is typical of European countries and Canada. Interestingly, productivity measurements suggest that these vacation periods enhance overall worker productivity.

With the introduction of these paid vacations, the French government developed the infrastructure to meet the needs of the vacationing population. Seaside resorts were built, the SNCF (French national train service) provide reduced fares during peak travel times to reduce car traffic, money is given to a wide range of cultural organizations to produce events for the tourist population, vacation villages were developed in the mountains to cater to the demand for outdoor activities.

As the French take to the beaches and mountains, businesses, stores and restaurants in the major cities may be closed. However, any enterprise catering to tourists will be open and busy. Fortunately, because Languedoc is such a prime vacation destination, it is unusual to find anything closed in the month of August.

∞

With vacation officially starting the first of August, the French frequently participate in a time-honoured tradition of *le grève* (strike). The ability for employees to strike was first conceived in 1791 and subsequently entrenched in laws, even within the European Union Charter of Rights. However, the restrictions of how strikes can be carried out are as regulated as the ability to strike. The traditional August strike is carried out by the SNCF and typically results in delays or cancelled trains. The government prohibits total shut down and strike plans must be submitted well in advance of any actions. Like so much of French life, there is a constant juggling between the rights of the citizen and the good of the community. The people most upset by this almost annual tradition are, as can be expected, foreign tourists. If train travel is part of your August holiday, it is advisable to have cancellation insurance and alternative travel options. Conversely, it can mean a chance to have an unplanned holiday and work on acquiring patience. In Languedoc, it is difficult to be stranded and not find the chance to discover new and unplanned travel memories.

∞

Much has been written about French women not getting fat but as Monique suggests, the real reason is that physical activity is such a part of everyone's routine. Beginning with primary school, exercise is built into daily schedules. Walking, hiking, swimming, cycling are activities that form part of the curriculum. Competitive sports are done outside of the school hours as private or school related events. This results in children developing life-long activities that form part of their everyday existence. As a result, great emphasis is placed on holiday excursions that involve these activities.

> Our friends arrived with their young children to spend time with us in August. Each morning, we would head out to a near-by park, beach or

forest. At first, we discovered that the children, ages 8 and 10, were not interested in the activities that we assumed, having watched Jean Luc's children next door, would have been exciting for them. Annick and Paul were typical French kids, outside every day after school cycling, working on a go-cart or playing hide and seek with other kids in the street. Finally, Monique told us how to improve the situation—invite Annick and Paul to join our young visitors. That morning, with four youngsters in tow, we set off for the Gorges d'Heric, a pleasant walk about 30 minutes from our house. The drive up to the base of the Gorges changes quickly from the rolling vineyards surrounding our villages to the valleys and granite outcrops of the Valley of the Orb river. The hamlet of Heric lies at the top of the gorge and is accessible by a now-paved narrow road from the village below. The climb snakes uphill quickly and inexperienced walkers stop to catch their breathe. Before long, our two young visitors were lagging behind as Annick and Paul clambered over the rocks and outcrops along the way. About a third of the way along, they told our young guests that there was a surprise in store for them around the next turn. Sure enough, lapping against the roadway was a pool of clear, mountain water. Because it was August, the temperature was most agreeable and before long all four of the children were in the shallow water, enjoying themselves as only children can. This broke the ice and from then on, all four of them were exploring the verges, scrambling across the stone bridge and up the ancient rock stairs on the other side of the gorge. By the time we reached the hamlet above, everyone was tuckered out—the children from playing hard and the adults from watching and sharing our own childhood adventures. Homemade ice cream and fruit drinks awaited us at the little stand at the top of the walk and as we sat and surveyed the view across the hills and down to the sea, we all appreciated the opportunity to be outside and explore. The walk down was easy and we marveled at the ages and robustness of so many of the *mamies* and *papies* (grandparents) that we met striding up the path or swimming in the pools.

The days passed quickly as we watched the four children engage so enthusiastically in the various outdoor activities we organized. Our young visitors returned home having made new friends, having experienced a range of activities that cost nothing but their willingness to participate and hopefully, acquired new skills that will stay with them. As I discussed the visit with Monique, she said that August is a good time to participate in French life with other families because the summer vacation is not particularly long compared to North America and being outdoors exploring the region is a favourite pastime.

Andrea Swan with Monique Guezel

∞

France has a transportation system that is the envy of many countries. Along with high speed trains, the TGV (train de grande vitesse) system, there are superhighways that lead from all parts of the north of France to the south. Low cost airlines, such as Ryanair, Easyjet and Air France HOP, service towns both large and small throughout Languedoc. In most of the summer season, fares are reasonable, trains are frequent, car rental hire is easy and traffic on the autoroutes is manageable. In August, however, things change as millions of tourists head to the beaches and the hills. Airline prices are at peak season rates so one must remember to book seats well in advance, trains are packed and the autoroutes on the first, mid and last weekends of the month are jammed with camping cars and holiday-makers. Therefore, coming in August requires extra planning regarding arrival and departure times. It's best to avoid Saturdays wherever possible as most rental homes do their changeover on that day which means that twice as many people are moving about.

Flying from Britain on Ryanair or Easyjet during the week can be relatively stress free if one remembers to book early. However, there is a limited baggage allowance and it is rather like travelling with a bunch of sardines as everyone is packed into the plane. There are numerous routes to all the cities in Languedoc so that it is usually possible to arrive close to your final destination.

Except for the frequent August 1st grève where the train union carries out rotating strikes, train service is otherwise excellent. Visitors from North America can book and print their train tickets from their home. Monique always reminds me that the schedules and prices for train tickets are posted only three months ahead of departure dates so one must plan to book quickly when the schedule appears if choice and price are an issue. There are a couple of considerations when booking that can reduce stress. It can sometimes be difficult to find a direct train so making sure that there is sufficient time to change trains can help make the voyage more pleasant. This is especially true in August when increased numbers of passengers can slow movement in the stations. There are two main options for buying tickets from North America. One is to use RailEurope and the other is to go directly to the SNCF website and book tickets for pickup in France. SNCF tickets tend to be cheaper but if trying to figure out how to get the tickets while in France seems like a hassle then RailEurope is a good choice.

> We typically fly into Paris and spend a few days exploring the city of lights. When it's time to head south, we pick up baguettes, fruit, pastries, meats and wine for our journey before heading over to the Gare de Lyon to board our TGV train car for a speedy but leisurely journey to Languedoc. To mark our transition, we frequently stop at Le Train Bleu, the Belle Epoque restaurant located in the Gare. This hidden treasure is a perfect sendoff to our trip south. As we head out of Paris, we are quickly moving through the rolling wheat fields of western Burgundy that slowly give way to the granite hills of the Massive Central. Then the sky changes

Andrea Swan with Monique Guezel

colour from light blue to deep azure, the granite hills slowly dissolve into limestone crags and the disappearing wheatfields are replaced with tidy rows of vines and lavender fields. We are almost home. The train chugs through the towns of Valence, Nîmes, Montpellier and along the coast through Sete and Agde before reaching our final stop. After four hours on the train, we are rested and have mentally transitioned from our North American high-energy life to the languid rhythm of Languedoc. Not even the busyness of August can dampen this experience.

Driving the autoroutes of France can be every wanna-bee racedrivers dream. The posted speed is 130 kilometers (80 MPH) per hour and in many cases that seems to be a suggestion as cars flash by you as you maintain the speed limit. However, there is now more vigilance on catching speed demons and fines are high. The newest autoroute is the A75 from Paris to Beziers and you can make the journey south in approximately 7 hours. The highway conditions are excellent on all autoroutes with frequent rest stops and clearly posted signage warning of any *bouchon* ahead (bottlenecks). Most autoroutes in France are toll routes but as the A75 was constructed to increase tourism to Languedoc, it is not tolled except for the bridge at Millau. The $10.00 charge for crossing the bridge seems like a small price to pay for such a major attraction. The toll costs along the A9 and the A61, the other autoroutes in the region, average $10.00 per 100 kilometers. It is important to have cash as often, the toll-booths do not accept North American credit or debit cards. The scenery can be interesting but there is little opportunity to see towns and villages as the highways are designed to pass around them. Monique talks about travelling up to the north of Paris and passing through the many picturesque towns of France. It does lengthen the journey but also the enhances memories of your travels. On Monique's advice, we try to do a combination of autoroutes and the RN (Route National) roads. These are secondary highways that pre-date the autoroutes. They are excellent and can be almost as fast if one travels during lunch or dinner hours. Monique warned us early on that the most dangerous time to travel in Languedoc is at 12:15PM when hungry Frenchmen are racing home for lunch. After a few close calls, we heed her advice.

> We were travelling down from Paris, part autoroute and part slow travel through villages of the Lyon region. We knew that the A75 was now open as far as Pezenas and so we connected to the A75 at Mende, heading towards Millau. We had heard the new bridge at Millau was an engineering wonder. Speeding along the busy highway, we turned the corner and before lay the most stunning sight. Tall, slender, blindingly white pillars strung out before us into infinity and from each pillar, like fine threads, were a series of wires suspending the pillars and the bridge surface in mid-air. The valley floor was somewhere beneath us but the clouds beneath the bridge blocked the view. We were driving "on air" into this magical scene. I have a significant

fear of heights but somehow I was transported both physically and spiritually along this route. It was breathtaking. We have been over it several times since our first trip and it never ceases to amaze me.

Driving in France, even in August is not difficult for an experienced driver. Cars are left hand drive the same as North America and all road signs are posted with international symbols. The most obvious difference is the frequent roundabouts that are used instead of stop signs at intersections. The car in the roundabout has priority and often there are multiple lanes so attention must be paid to cars on all sides changing lanes and exiting the roundabout. One advantage to roundabouts is that if you can't figure out which exit you need, just keep driving around the circle until you find your way. In towns and villages, unless there is a yield or stop sign, drivers coming in on your right have the right of way. This can be nerve-wracking and while it is being phased out, it is best to be cautious especially where streets are narrow, in rural areas or where foreigners are infrequent. As Monique says, there is nothing like having a tractor coming out of a side road with no evidence of slowing down and assuming the right of way to spoil a pleasant afternoon drive in the country.

French drivers may seem reckless and road signs may look like they are used as mere suggestions but the laws are very clear and driving on any highway is easy if certain rules are respected. On four lane divided highways, the passing lane can only be used to pass so it is normal to see drivers move into and out of the passing lane as they pass cars and trucks. On three lane autoroutes, trucks are only allowed in the slow, right hand lane except to pass. They are not allowed in the inside passing lane that is reserved for cars travelling at high speed. For drivers uncertain of the rules, it is acceptable to stay in the truck lane as long as the traffic flow is being maintained. Of course, at peak times in August, the autoroutes can be so choked with traffic that no one is moving quickly.

In August, the roads are very busy especially at peak time of rush hour, late afternoon as everyone heads home or to the beaches and on Saturdays. This is the time to explore the back roads of Languedoc. All of France has been mapped out in great detail and the IGN topographical maps provide incredible detail of even the smallest lanes and trails. Along with Michelin maps, they are available at tabacs and grocery stores and are a good resource for exploring areas on foot, by car or bicycle. When the rest of the world is stranded on the autoroute in the heat of August, you can be winding your way along the byways of Languedoc in search of your destination.

∞

Over the decades, the French government has supported the development of vacation villages along the coast and close to various national parks. Throughout the spring and early summer, highway traffic is peppered with flat bed trucks carrying holiday homes to be installed in these parks. These prefab cottages will form extensive villages providing a complete, all-inclusive vacation option for families. They are very popular with French families as they offer an extensive array of activities and a complete break from work and school routine. For the visitor from another country, they can offer a good alternative for being immersed in a French environment.

∞

August in Languedoc will be peak season for mountain hiking and camping with Languedoc covered with GR routes (Grande Randonées) and the shorter PR routes (Promenades et Randonées). The FFRP (French Hiking association) is the best resource for walkers and hikers and their Topoguides are excellent. Volunteers ensure that trails and signage are kept up to date. The main GR routes through Languedoc are the GR7 and the GR36 that wind their way through some of the greatest wilderness territory in France. There are campsites, hostels, B&B, farm gites and small hotels that cater to hikers. However, just as with any tourist activity in August, careful planning and pre-booking is a must. Camping in the wild is tolerated in France for overnight camping but it is wise to be aware of any restrictions or concerns such as wild boar and hunters.

While the long distance Grande Randonée routes are the preferred venue for the seasoned hiker, the local PR routcs are frequently used by novice or amateur hikers including families. It is a common site to see young children ambling along with parents and grandparents down the trails and roads. In almost any small village in the Haute Languedoc, one can spot the yellow, red or white markers that are the international signage of walking routes. These often long-established trails lead into the countryside and connect communities throughout the region. Another set of signposts are often accompany the PR and GR routes are the VTT signs. These refer to mountain bike routes so it is possible to be walking along and have a cyclist fly by you on the trail. These VTT trails are designed and maintained by the French Federation of Cycling.

∞

Beach life in August is a study in cultural habits. It is easy to spot the recent arrivals from the north with their white skin slowly turning red in the high noon sun. From morning to early afternoon, the typical beach visitors are tourists from other countries trying to get a head start on their tans or more likely, sunburns. Beach shops cater to this crowd with an extensive variety of food, beverage, clothing and sporting gear stores. Increasingly, there are businesses providing wind surfing, sailing, diving, snorkeling, fishing lessons, excursions and rentals. By the mid-afternoon, these tourists are heading home to nurse their burns and start on afternoon activities around the campground or rental home. The next wave will be the French tourists who come prepared to take advantage of evening entertainment, beach picnics and the warmer, late afternoon sun. Finally, the local French families will arrive having had their main meal and siesta earlier in the day and are now arriving for a final swim, walk or late meal.

For the newcomer to French beaches, one of the most disconcerting images may be that of women going topless on the beach. It probably corresponds to the more laid back French attitude to sexuality in other areas. It is interesting to note that while French woman may go topless, they are more discerning as to whether they have the figure to be topless. One is likely to see more indiscriminant toplessness during the morning beach crowds when tourists think it's the "in thing" to do.

Languedoc beaches are known for their miles of sandy, shallow edges where children can frolic safely. Numerous rock breakwaters have been created to provide calm, warm pools close to shore. However, in August, finding your small piece of beach can be daunting. Away from the Mediterranean beaches there are numerous, excellent lakes and rivers that can provide cooling relief from the hot sun.

∞

August is one long festival with every imaginable event going on in towns and villages throughout all but the most remote parts of the region. One of the highlights of the August festival season is the water jousting tournaments in Sete. First held in 1666 to commemorate the completion of the Canal du Midi, this festival focuses on the jousting tournaments held on the canals of Sete. Although matches will happen throughout July and August, the final competitions for the Gold Cup are held during the week-long feast of St. Louis in late August. The matches use large, brightly decorated, red or blue wooden boats manned by ten fishermen and a captain, all dressed in immaculate white uniforms and representing their local communities. Blue boats traditionally signified bachelors and the red boats the married men though today those lines are blurred. Each boat has a *tintaine* (protruding ladder-like platform) on the bow on which the jouster and his helpers perch with the jouster holding his 9 foot long, iron tipped wooden spear in one hand and his 28 inch wooden breastplate across his other arm. As the boats are rowed as close to each other as possible, the jouster will attempt to dislodge his opponent from the other boat into the water. The skill lies in being able to push your opponent into the water without loosing your own balance. Remarkably, the boat crew includes an oboist and a drummer playing a traditional tune just as the jousters prepare for combat and the music will continue until someone has been dislodged into the water. You can imagine the atmosphere with local bands on the quai rallying the crowds as the boats begin their battle. Crowds clog the stands, restaurants, canals and streets to view the spectacle and participate with shouts and applause. Fuelled by Pastis, rosé and the seafood specialties of Sete, the atmosphere is electric as the competition reaches its climax and a final "king" is declared. Braving the traffic, hoards and heat of August is justified in having the chance to participate in this truly Languedocienne festival. August in Languedoc, especially along the coast, is a festival atmosphere on steroids. However, your patience will be rewarded with the chance to participate in French life enjoying the full flavour of Languedoc. Stories of traffic jams, dense crowds, amazing festivals and sites will make your travel memories all the more colourful.

∞

When we were discussing recipes for August, Monique talked about the heat of summer and how the meals tended either to be cold, prepared in advance recipes or else "grillades" meat or fish that can grilled on a barbecue. She indicated that people who live in Languedoc tend to remain close to home during the month as the roads and tourist areas are too full of visitors and it's too hot to be outside for long unless one has a swimming pool. Her favourite recipes tend to be based on grains such as rice, lentils and beans with whatever fresh vegetables Pierre brings in fresh from the garden. After an early morning walk up the hill to the markets to check out what is fresh, she can then plan her menu. This basic recipe allows so many variations that it's easy to get through the month with a minimal use of the stove.

MONIQUE'S BASIC ONE DISH SUMMER MEAL

Ingredients for 4 persons:

2 cups of cooked lentils, rice, beans, pasta
or any other grain that you want

Combination of diced onions, tomatoes, shredded carrots or beets, peppers, cucumbers, beans,
radishes or whatever else may be fresh

Additional items that make for an interesting flavour
are olives, sliced palm hearts, artichoke hearts, grated
celeriac or jicama, fennel, apples, pears, nuts.

Any protein you choose. Monique's favourites are smoked
duck breast, cold roasted chicken, cooked chicken livers,
cold meats, tuna, hard boiled eggs, variety of cheeses.

Lettuce or other greens

Vinaigrette

Preparation:

Combine the grains and vegetables in a large serving bowl and toss with a vinaigrette suited to the foods in the salad. This can be made in the morning and kept cool.

Wash the lettuce or other leaves and place in a large bowl

Just before serving, add the protein source to the mix grain and vegetables and toss lightly.

Serve by placing the lettuce leaves on each plate and top with the grain and vegetable mixture

Add fresh bread and wine for a light, summer meal

OMELETTE

When I suggested to Monique that we prepare an omelette, she seemed surprised that such a basic recipe would need to be included in a book. When I explained that French omelettes taste so different from ones I prepare at home, she agreed to show me how to prepare a classic French omelette à la Monique.

Ingredients for 2 persons:

4 fresh eggs at room temperature

1 tablespoon unsalted butter

Salt and pepper or "herbes fines" – combination of finely minced chives, tarragon, parsley and chervil

Preparation:

Beat the 4 eggs briskly so that the yolks and whites are well combined with no stringy bits.

Add pinches of salt and pepper or herbes fines

A non-stick skillet works best to cook the omelettes

Place tablespoon of unsalted butter in the skillet and place over medium to high heat. Gas heat is one of Monique's secrets to an evenly cooked omelette. When I tested the recipe at home, I found that cooking it over the gas side burner of the BBQ produced a better result than using the electric stove.

Pour egg mixture into the skillet and continuously and slowly stir with a fork. The cooking process should take only a couple of minutes so that the eggs are light and airy with no lumps or overcooked areas. When the omelette appears ready, turn one side over the other and then using a plate, turn the omelette out onto a plate, ready to serve. A classic French omelet looks slightly moist when it's ready.

Monique explained that if I wanted to add fillings, it should be done while the omelette is flat in the skillet, before turning it over.

After a tiring day at the beach, this is a perfect, quick evening meal and all it needs is fresh bread and a green salad.

GRILLADES

In almost any house with a backyard in Languedoc there is often a large stone grill made out of local stone or concrete blocks. Unlike barbeques, these grills typically use wood as the fuel source although some are now equipped with propane. Monique explained that the best grillades are cooked with wood and that the secret to a good fire starts with branches from the *sarments*, the dried grape vines cut from last years pruning or dried, wild rosemary that has been gathered on walks up into the hills These give a unique flavour to the foods being cooked.

Like Monique's basic one dish meal, her recommendations for a grillade reflect what is fresh at the butcher, from the fisherman and at the vegetable stand. Typical foods include brochettes, foods combined on a skewer, whole vegetables such as zucchini, onion, tomato or eggplant, fish and seafood and all sorts of meats. Monique used skewers of rosemary and thyme branches when we prepared lamb brochettes. She used tarragon and fennel branches for the fish. In both cases, the delicate taste of the herbs infused the lamb and fish.

Cooking directions for grillades are the same as for any barbecue recipe. I have been able to translate Monique's suggestions for brochettes, grilled vegetables and meats into excellent meals using our propane barbecue at home. My secret is getting my husband to do the cooking as I would never pretend to understand how to adjust BBQ temperatures.

POULET ROTI

Poulet Roti (roast chicken) is a classic French discovery that is a must for the hot days of August. Monique was clear that this is one recipe that is best left to the experts, especially during the heat of August. Every market, butcher or supermarket has a free-standing rotisserie with whole chickens slowly turning and basting in their own juices. The knowing shopper arrives at the market and immediately places an order for a chicken to be picked up later in the morning. At noon, it is easy to find the way to the Poulet Roti stand because the smell wafts over the heads of the crowds, pulling you enticingly forward. After picking up fresh produce for a simple salad, a baguette made with artisanal flour, a couple of cheeses, some fresh figs and melons that are now appearing at the fruit stalls and of course, a simple tarte for dessert, there is nothing to be done but to head home and enjoy the meal under the protection of a large shade tree.

PANACHÉ

This easy to prepare drink is a great thirst-quencher during the hot days of August. It's part beer and part lemonade. I have had it served with lemonade and also with Sprite and both are refreshing. The French use a blonde beer such as Stella Artois rather than a dark beer. I find that $1/4$ to $1/2$ beer to lemonade is enough to minimize the sweetness of the lemonade and prevent any alcohol buzz.

SEPTEMBER

le vendange, Canal de Midi, cycling, boules, rugby

Ah, September in Languedoc. Warm, lazy afternoons, no crowds, children back in school and the air heavy with the smell of ripening grape clusters. This is the month to motor slowly along the Canal du Midi, stopping off at each village or Auberge to sample the wines and foods on offer. It's the time to join grape pickers and experience the back-breaking work of getting in the harvest and then taking part in the evening feast with the fading sun working its magic on your sore, aching muscles-or is that the wine?

For any sports enthusiast, September is a good month to check out the spectator sport of rugby for which Languedoc is justly famous. It is also the chance to check out sports events that are typical in Languedoc such as boules, or le tabourine. And of course, there is the usual array of sports activities available for the visitor to try in a region that places a high emphasis on physical fitness. The long, hot days of summer have warmed the Mediterranean and swimming is now at its best as the beaches are less crowded and yet the sand and water are warm and the resort towns are still brimming with activity.

∞

The Canal du Midi is a 200 kilometer navigational waterway that runs from Agde to Toulouse where it connects to the Garonne River on its journey to the Atlantic via Bordeaux. Construction started in 1666 under the supervision of Paul Riquet, a native of Beziers. The concept of linking the Mediterranean wo the Atlantic had been considered for hundreds of years dating back to the Romans but it was Riquet who figured out how to manage the water supply necessary to maintain adequate water levels in the canal. The intention was to use this marine short cut to move grain and wine more safely and quickly to markets rather than go around Spain and the Strait of Gibralter. By 1850, railroads and highways were taking their toll on the waterway business and by 1970 all freight traffic ended. Now it is used for tourism, recreation and housing. With a slow, meandering rhythm and 91 locks to navigate, the canal offers the opportunity to escape into another world. One of the beauties of the canal is the plane trees that line both sides of the towpaths. First planted shortly after construction of the canal, these trees with their massive canopy of leaves offer shade from the hot sun of the south. They provide a dappled light and give an ever-changing glimmer to the water ahead. As the result of a fungus growth, many of them are being replaced but efforts are underway to restore the banks to their previous beauty. Boating on the canal is truly a sensuous experience, being gently carried along the calm waterway, seeing the natural wonders of the region in an unhurried journey to the next lock or village, smelling and tasting the fare at the numerous restaurants, markets and auberges that line the canal. The boats on the canal range from large, renovated Dutch barges to powerboats or small British style narrow boats. With the increasing demand, there are now a few hotel boats that cater to those who wish a completely pampered experience. Along the canal are several points where one can arrange boat rentals for self-guided holidays. The boats are well designed for even the novice sailor and crew. Rental periods can be daily, weekend or longer so are available for anyone to book during a visit to Languedoc. One note of caution is that this is no speedy trip; one should plan to travel only a few miles per day in order to appreciate the experience.

For our second trip on the Canal du Midi, we decided to rent a narrow boat and travel along the canal from Le Somail to Poilhes and back, a total distance of 31 miles over four days. Our boat of choice was a narrow boat, designed and built in England. The young couple at the boat rental agency were delightful and gave us tons of good information, including who had the best baguettes and where to find the best restaurants along our way. We headed out in the late September afternoon as most others had moored and were settling back for their aperos. The atmosphere along the canal, especially in September, is relaxed as there is no rush to find a mooring with the reduced number of boaters. We were soon tied up to one of the iron bollocks located along the bank and settled in to enjoy the afternoon glow from the setting sun. Wine and nibbles always seem to taste better in these surroundings. That evening, we were lulled to sleep by the gentle movement of the current but were rudely awakened by the early morning shrill call of the crows and magpies along the bank. Meals were a delightful combination of fresh foods picked up at the morning markets along the banks and the provisions that we had brought along. We all agreed that the work of cruising slowly along does manage to work up a large appetite. Every so often we were put to work as we navigated the locks. Normally, each lock can hold several boats depending on their size. Squeezing in alongside a massive Dutch barge is no mean feat. Ropes most be tied and untied with a rapidity and dexterity that can be nerve-wracking but we soon became comfortable with the techniques and did not lose any fingers. At one point in the journey, my husband and I were cycling along the towpath as the other couple maneuvered our boat along the canal when we spotted a large Dutch barge bearing the familiar name of Linquenda. We had been on a boat named Linquenda several years previously. Could this possibly be the same one? We scrambled down the bank and boldly introduced ourselves to the owner who informed us that "yes" this was indeed the same Linquenda that had provided us with such pleasurable memories. He kindly showed us around and over drinks and then dinner, we all shared stories of our travels. He spoke little English but between the five of us, we managed to convey information, jokes and friendship. The slow and quiet pace of life on the canal offers opportunities for just such pleasures. Over the centuries, side canals and an inland link to the Rhone were added to now make it possible to travel throughout all of France on a web of canals and rivers.

∞

September is the height of grape harvest time and offers the best chance to participate in a working holiday. The vines are heavy with swollen grapes, the gardens are bursting with freshness and people are ready to roll up their shirtsleeves to help. The various grape varieties all have different harvesting times so there is always a good chance that one can participate in the *vendange* (harvest). Monique carefully explained the process for harvesting: typically, the earlier the vines are pruned is an indication of how early the grapes will be harvested. Some of the white varieties even harvest at night to take advantage of increased sugar levels. Many of the red varieties such as Grenache, Cinsault and Merlot are harvested in September with the more robust reds such as Syrah and Cabernet Sauvignon left until October. There are increasing opportunities for even the casual visitor to help out during the vendange. The best way to find out about this is to check out the local newspaper, the Midi Libre or the local tourist information offices. If the village is too small, the Mairie (Town Hall) will be the place to check. If you are staying at a B&B in a village, they will likely know what is available. Remember, however, that if you commit to help, be prepared to carry through as the owner is relying on your willing hands. Often, local country B&Bs offer a chance for guests to help on their vineyard as part of the rental package.

∞

Languedoc is full of volunteer opportunities and the best source of information is *WWOOF* (Willing Workers on Organic Farms). This international organization connects volunteers to people who need help on farms. It can provide a low-cost, different vacation experience. Basically, the volunteer provides time and willing hands in exchange for room and board. WWOOF ensures that the working and living conditions are safe and reasonable. It is an ideal chance to live in a rural environment in the south of France. There are minimum stay times and the worker must be fit enough to participate as needed. The range of possibilities should meet anyone's needs. The basic tenets of WWOOF of "Trust, Tolerance and Generosity" underline the value of this type of holiday.

∞

For the past thirty years, France has set aside the third weekend in September for *Les Jours Patromonie* (Heritage Days). During this time, chateaus, historical buildings and artifacts not normally opened to the public present tours and exhibits for the local population. In our small village, the local chateau of the *patron* (family of the historical lord of the village) is opened for everyone to visit. It is seen as an important chance to "see how the other half lives". Information is published in the local newspaper of all the openings and exhibits.

Monique told us that the chateau of La Famille Esteve would be open on the upcoming weekend and encouraged us to visit. As we approached the front door, we were met by M le Conte, looking suave in his fine suit and the cravet knotted at his throat. He did not look overly thrilled to have *les paysans* traipse through the house. It was interesting to note that while France is a strong social democratic country, the class structure of aristocrats and peasants still lingers.

∞

If lying on a sandy beach is more your style, then Languedoc with 200 kilometers of seashore should fill the bill. From the beach resorts of La Grande Motte near Montpellier through to the western resort of Port Leucate, these self-contained villages were designed specifically as holiday destinations. In the 1950s, President DeGaulle established the mandatory four week summer holiday and in 1960 encouraged the creation of holiday villages to meet the needs of a growing population. La Grande Motte was created from scratch along the coast of the Mediterranean and is totally integrated to meet the needs of a holiday clientele. The architecture of the development has withstood the test of time and remains an iconic sight along the horizon from Montpellier. Other seaside holiday villages also sprang up over the decades but grew more as extensions of existing fishing villages. Because June and September are considered the "shoulder months" of the tourist season, apartment and house rentals can be a bargain at this time.

September was unusually warm as we headed to Cap d'Agde to visit friends who had rented a holiday apartment, a short block from the beaches. The shops were all open plying their bikinis, sunglasses and towels to the remaining holiday makers. Clearly, the crowd had thinned and aged from August providing a much more relaxed atmosphere. We joined Marie at the beach and swan the afternoon away in warm seawater that washed over the hot sands. Compared to our visit in May, the water temperature was wonderful. After a stroll for an afternoon gelati, we walked along the seawall towards the unprotected area of Cap d'Agde. We could have walked almost clear to Spain but the bars were opening for "aperos" and it was time to be moving on as the afternoon "passage" was beginning where people come out to stroll the boardwalks and bask in the late afternoon rays.

When Monique heard that we were going to Cap d'Agde for the day, she chuckled and proceeded to give us a heads up on what we might expect. Cap d'Agde is famous for a special beach area and this reputation has an international renown. One must be careful saying that one is spending time in Cap d'Agde as it is the nudist capital of Europe. In the late 1940's, German tourists arrived in the area and nude sunbathing became the order of the day. The impoverished owner of the land realized that it would be more profitable to move from olive growing to developing accommodation for the nudist camp and promptly formalized the camping arrangements. Since then, the *naturiste* (nudist) area has grown into a major tourist area with rules of nudity as the norm. In addition, part of the area has become an international "swingers" colony where anything goes. Cap D'Agde Naturiste Village is now a completely self-contained village with all amenities and welcomes up to 10,000 tourists in August. While there are other small naturiste camps throughout Languedoc, this one is certainly the largest and best known.

> We were driving around on one of our usual Sunday afternoon explorations of the region when we saw the sign for the "Parc Naturiste" and decided to explore what we assumed was a regional park. It was obviously well known as there were several other cars parked near the park entrance. As we walked into the park area, we were surprised to find a gate and fencing leading into the area. It was when we came to the large information board that our suspicions were aroused as we deciphered in our halting French the rules and regulations regarding the park. Realizing our mistake that this was in fact, a nudist park, we quickly made it back to our car, laughing at our naivete and the need to improve our French. We now remind friends that when visiting Cap d'Agde, "naturiste" does not mean a "nature reserve" or one can find themselves seeing more than they wanted.

For the cycling enthusiast, Languedoc is full of rigourous mountain climbs that should test any cyclist. From the Pyrenèes to the Cevennes, from the narrow, winding roads of the villages in the Haute Languedoc to the long, slow roads leading down from the Montagne Noire and the quiet, country roads leading out from most villages, there is something for ever level of cyclist. However, Languedoc does seem to draw the Tour de France wannebees. No Sunday drive into the hills is complete without coming across the local cycling clubs out for their weekend trials. Dressed in colourful spandex and helmets, these riders come careening down the snake-like roads at breakneck speed, daring the motorist to move to the shoulder. These are not twenty-something athletes but are fit seniors who take this sport seriously. For the avid visiting cyclist, it is possible to join these Sunday tours by checking out the local papers on Friday or Saturday for information on the upcoming rides. Typically, the ride ends at a local bar for a recap of the day's events.

> As we rounded the corner, snaking up along the road from the valley of the Orb River to the Montagne Noire, we came face to face with a *peloton* (riding group) of Sunday cyclists flying down before us. We veered to the curbside as they careened by, not in a reckless way but clearly skilled at negotiating the narrow, mountain roads full of Sunday drivers. After steadying our nerves, we continued along our way only to encounter three more troupes of riders. Our

lazy Sunday drive was becoming rather harrowing! Later, as we made our way back home and stopped in the village for *un pression* (beer on tap), we met up with the first group of cyclists. To our astonishment, these were not joy-riding teens out for a thrill; these were seasoned men, well past their prime. However, they were so fit and energetic, so experienced in cycling these hills that neither we nor they were likely in any great danger of a major collision.

Rugby is considered the "national sport" of Languedoc and the Toulouse club is one of the most successful in Europe. Even small towns will be part of a regional rugby league with Beziers featuring an excellent stadium and home to a national level team. The Top 14 rugby season starts in mid-August so September is a good time to catch some of the action featuring Montpellier, Toulouse, Perpignan and Castres. For lower league matches, it is easy to catch a game almost any day of the week somewhere in Languedoc. Competition is fierce with local towns having excellent rugby schools that often provide the new players for national teams. One friend's main reason for visiting us was because our village rugby team was excellent and games promised to be exciting.

Our village team was playing in front of the home crowd and the rugby field was full of supporters. It was our first rugby match but no one had prepared us for the clamour, colour and general mayhem that awaited us. And that was the spectators! Watching rugby is not for the faint of heart. The action always seems to be one step away from an all out brawl with kicking, hitting and pushing part of the action. Unlike the protective gear worn by hockey or football players, these guys look more like Roman gladiators in their short shorts and t-shirts. Broken bones are a badge of honour and few games end without some form of injury. Between the crowds and the loudspeakers, the noise becomes an expected part of the game. I suspect that the atmosphere at a rugby game in Languedoc is reminiscent of the games held in the Roman coliseums of long ago.

For a more relaxing Languedoc sport boules or le tambourin are great opportunities to watch the French at play. Boules is a cousin of bocce ball and petanque with variations in the number of players, number of balls and construction of the balls. It is somewhat similar to lawn bowling or curling. In all cases, it is played wherever the group can find some open ground so no special pitches or rinks are needed. In almost all towns and villages in Languedoc, there is at least one boules pitch where the community gathers to either play or watch. Boules is as central to the south of France as sunshine, Pastis and plane trees. For the interested spectator the rules of the game are simple: the object of the game is to get the metal balls as close to the *cochon* (small wooden ball) as possible. The team with the most balls closest wins the round. The hard part of the game is that the cochon moves with every round so the terrain is constantly changing. Unlike curling or shuffleboard, this constant changing adds a challenge to the play. Also unlike these other games, the conversations, the apparel and the antics create quite a different experience.

Monique alerted us to the monthly tournament of the local boules club where her son, Philipe was playing. We sauntered over and found the action well underway. There were at least twenty different boules games going on in the small, confined space under the massive plane trees. It was difficult to make out who belonged to which team as the players wove in and out. The cochons were sometimes so close to each other that balls were in danger of being played for other teams. The vast majority of players were elderly men although a few teams had token women who did not appear to be the lead players. It was evident from the discussions and the looks on everyone's faces that this was serious business. The lay of the land was examined, measurements were taken to determine the distance needed for the take-out shot, heads bent closely to discuss the shot. Then the real examination took place when measurements were done to determine the closest ball to the cochon. Winning points were not claimed without a discussion. After the decisions had been taken, balls were retrieved for the next round. We watched as elderly men dropped a string to the ground and their balls magically popped up for them to grab. It took a moment to realize that on the end of the string was a magnet, making the task all the easier. As with so many events in Languedoc, the day ended with a verre d'amitie as the exploits and winning strategies of the game were dissected.

La Tambourin is a game that is unusual and found only in a few places in Languedoc. This game likely originated in mid-1600 and has roots in jeu de paume, tennis and an Italian game called tambuello. Today, the game is played on a large court with five players on each team using a handheld *tambourin* (without the musical jangles on the sides). The main towns where games are held are Pezenas, Gignac, Florensac. Numerous other small towns that dot the coast of Languedoc often have tambourin courts. Be ready for a fast paced game where skilled players send the ball shooting back and forth across the open court.

∞

For September, Monique chose three recipes that might well be served to hungry workers at the end of a hard day of picking grapes. They are all filling and also use up the mountains of zucchini that are now ready for harvest.

RATATOUILLE

This classic southern French dish is best prepared when all the fresh ingredients are in the market. Like so many French dishes, there are variations but in a vrai ratatouille, the eggplant and zucchini should be cooked separately and then the other vegetables are cooked together. After the Thursday market and a chat with Bernadette, I came home with my basket laden with onions from Nezignan le Cebe, eggplant, peppers and zucchini from a local farmer, violet garlic from Cadours and tomatoes from Pierre's garden. The thyme would come from my own small herb garden. Monique indicated that she uses canned tomatoes when the ones in the market are not at their peak or are not local. This is a great dish to make in large quantities as it mellows with time and can be served either cold or warm, as a main dish or as a side.

I asked Monique why one had to cook the eggplant separately from the zucchini but could combine the other ingredients. She said that it was important to treat each vegetable according to its needs. Eggplant must be skinned and cooked separately to allow the inner juices to absorb the liquids on their own and not compete with other vegetables. Her careful dicing of the eggplant was deliberate to ensure that all the cubes were uniform. Her preparing of the garlic was so different from my haphazard approach or the modern techniques I've watched on television. No fancy garlic press for her as she carefully minced the heads into miniscule bits with her sharp knife. I have come to appreciate the lessons I am learning from her about food preparation, where the food comes from, the work involved in growing and harvesting it and the care and diligence one should take when preparing meals. This was so different from my North American experience where the mantra is "time is money" and the more shortcuts to a meal, the better. I am learning to slow down, attend to the matter at hand and to be intentional in carrying out any task I do.

Ingredients for 4 Persons:

2 onions

2 small eggplants

2 medium zucchini

2 loves garlic

1 large red pepper

500 ml of canned diced tomatoes or
5 fresh medium tomatoes

Few sprigs of fresh thyme

Salt and pepper to taste

Several tablespoons of olive oil

Preparation:

Peel eggplant then cut lengthwise into a least four strips then cut into small cubes.

Place cubed eggplant into a casserole pot with several table-spoons olive oil and 2-3 grinds of salt and pepper. Cook covered over low heat for 5-10 minutes until eggplant is soft and mushy. Remove from pot and set aside.

Peel zucchini lengthwise leaving alternate rows of peel. Slice into lengths then cube into small pieces. Put into pot with 1 tablespoon of olive oil. Cook covered over low heat for 5-10 minutes until zucchini is soft. Remove from pot and set aside. Add to eggplant.

Dice onions and chop garlic finely. Add to pot with 1 tablespoon olive oil.

Remove stem and seeded from red pepper and cut into small pieces. Add to onion mix and cook until soft.

Monique showed me a trick for quickly stemming and removing the seeds. She pushes the stem down into the middle of the pepper with her thumb. She then cuts open the pepper and the stem and seeds fall away.

When the onion and pepper mix are cooked, add in the eggplant and zucchini, stirring together.

Add the tomatoes. If Monique is using fresh tomatoes, she cuts the tomato in half and grate each half to easily remove the pulp.

Add the thyme and more salt and pepper.

Continue cooking over *un petit feu* (a low heat) for at least 30 minutes and watch carefully that the mixture doesn't burn.

This recipe can easily be doubled and it great cold or hot.

ENDIVES AUX JAMBONS (ENDIVES WITH HAM)

Ingredients:

4 medium size Belgian endives

4 slices of ham

¼ cup butter

4 tablespoons flour

2 cups milk

1 ½ cups shredded Emmental or Gruyere cheese

Salt & pepper

Preparation:

Cut out a small cone from the flat end of each endive. Be careful not to cut too much as the leaves will fall off.

Put endives in salted water and simmer gently for 45 minutes until a knife easily pierces the cut end. It is good to cook them several hours ahead or the day before and let them sit before using.

Wrap each endive in a slice of ham and place in a casserole dish.

Bechamel Sauce:

Melt butter over low heat and add the flour until you have a thick paste.

Slowly whisk in the milk and salt and pepper. Cook over low heat, stirring constantly until mixture thickens to consistency of a crème soup. Add 1 cup cheese and continue stirring until mixture is thick and cheese melted.

Pour over endives Sprinkle remaining cheese over mixture.

Bake at 350°F until golden. This dish reheats well and flavours improve.

POTATO-ZUCCHINI GRATIN

Monique suggested this dish when I was trying to prepare a meal for guests arriving the next day. I have to admit that I was a bit skeptical about how tasty potatoes and zucchini could be but even Pierre, Monique's husband assured me that it was delicious. This is a perfect buffet dish and is great cold or hot as we discovered on our subsequent picnic.

Ingredients for 4 persons:

> 3 large potatoes
>
> 3 zucchini
>
> 3 eggs
>
> ¼ cup butter
>
> 4 tablespoons crème fraiche
>
> 2 cups grated Gruyere cheese
>
> Salt and pepper to taste
>
> 1 teaspoon grated nutmeg

Preparation:

Peel and cube potatoes and cook in boiling salted water until soft

Peel zucchini lengthwise alternating a green strip with a peeled strip-Monique says that all the best cooks in the village leave zucchini and eggplant partially unpeeled to give flavour and colour to a dish. When finished peeling, cut into cubes.

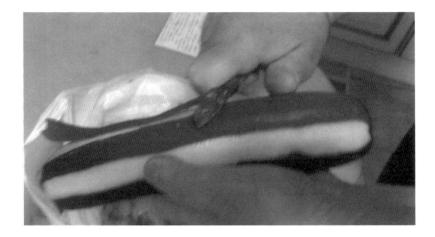

When potatoes are cooked, drain and add zucchini to potato water to cook until soft

Put all ingredients together into a large bowl, blender or food processor. Puree mixture until smooth. Put into large baking dish, bake until top is dark golden approximately 45-60 minutes. The gratin should be firm to the touch. Bake longer if needed. Serve hot or cold. This is a good vegetarian recipe and can be easily pared with a salad.

OCTOBER

*celebrations of harvests, health care, hidden
vineyards, food festivals, culinary talents*

The reddening leaves are slowly falling from the trees and vines now and the pomegranates and quince are beginning to stand out among the bare branches of the trees. Autumn in Languedoc is on its way. The streets and fields are quieter now as the vendange is almost over and it is time to enjoy the fruits of one's labours before the darkness of winter descends.

Languedoc days still hold their warmth and the evenings continue to be light well into the later hours. Children are back in school and the first *jours de scolaire* (school holidays) are about to begin. The Mediterranean is still warm enough to swim in if you enjoy lake temperature water and the bars and cafes along the promenades are open and offer a quiet respite. The one drawback to October is that the "rainy season", those two weeks of intermittent showers that cloud the month, may begin so an umbrella is a must. However, the air is warm and the rains pass quickly, just long enough to slip into a local bar for a quick *café normal* (espresso). October is the time to visit if you want to participate in the village celebrations of *le primeur* (first tasting of the new wine), celebrate the harvests of the chestnuts and hazelnuts, visit the massive antique festival called le "Grand déballage (the big sweep) in Pezenas and the participate in the autumn festival season from mid-October to mid-November.

∞

We have read numerous reviews comparing health care among leading developed countries of the world, and in almost all of them, health care in France comes out on top on several indicators including life expectancy, cost, access and quality of treatments. But what does that mean for a visitor? There are several points to consider: emergency and intensive care is excellent and is, except in isolated villages, readily available. Languedoc is home to the oldest medical school in the western world in Montpellier and it has continued to excel in a wide variety of specialties. Doctors, visiting nurses and physiotherapists are part of a committed approach to keeping people in their homes. There is no cost to the patient, including visitors, for newly diagnosed cancer treatment, accident and trauma care or acute medical emergencies. While visitors are wise to have travel insurance, there is no fear that you will need extraordinary coverage in the event of a serious medical issue. In addition, dental care is excellent and dental emergencies are quickly attended to; pharmacists will typically refill prescriptions for medications for chronic diseases as long as the pill bottle has all the information and the medication is available in France; ambulance and fire teams are highly trained and physicians ride along in ambulances for rapid response. Even in our small village, there are three family physicians, three visiting nurse offices, a physiotherapist and two dental offices.

> I woke up one morning with an eye infection and walked along to the local physician. As is frequently the case, he does not book appointments, you simply show up and await your turn. There is no receptionist, the physician greeted me in halting English and brought me into the examining room. After the consultation, he wrote out a prescription and a bill for the visit and sent me on my way. The office visit was 23 euros or about $34 and the antibiotic eye ointment was $2.75.

> France is working to increase the use of telemedicine especially for small villages to have access to specialists. A friend visited his physician and as part of the physical examination, the doctor moved a small object across his chest and then placed it on his computer terminal. The images were immediately transmitted sent electronically to a cardiologist in Paris who read the information and prepared the report for the family doctor sitting in his small office in the village.

We continue to hear stories of state of the art care, treatments and results which leave us confident that if one should be ill in France, the response to treatment will be swift and effective and the bill will not be crippling.

∞

By early October, most of the vendange has finished and the early morning tractor sounds are gone. The heavy perfume of the grapes still hangs in the warm air and walking through the vineyards, one can still find a few remaining grape clusters to sample. There may even be some vineyards still fully laden with fruit—these will be the heavy reds such as Syrah, Carignan and Mourvedre. The sun stills holds its heat with temperatures in the low to mid twenties (mid-seventies F). Walking out among the vines, one is likely to meet others either working or appreciating that their hard work is finished for another year.

It wasn't often that we visited France in October but on our arrival, Monique asked if we were interested in helping with the harvest. The temperature was absolutely perfect but rain was predicted in a few days so time was of the essence. Rising early the next morning, we were in the vineyard by 7:30 AM, gloves and hats on and clippers in hand. The technique is not difficult if you don't mind bending at the waist or squatting for hours on end! Most branches have only a couple of large, ripe, juicy grape clusters hanging down beneath their leaf canopy. The trick is to cut off each one without nicking oneself and place it in a pail or basket. We were happy to be out in the sunshine, helping our neighbour and having the chance to contribute to the grape harvest as we had often been the recipients of the results. However, we weren't entirely sure what we had gotten ourselves into to. We are urban dwellers after all. Mid-morning, the gong sounded and we all headed under the olive trees where coffee and a quick *goutée* (sweet snack) awaited us. Although we were happy to stand around and chat with new friends, Joelle gently reminded us of the work to be done ahead of us. By now, the sun was climbing steadily as were the temperatures; shirts and jeans were doffed for t-shirts and shorts as we again turned our attention to the work at hand. It seemed hours before the gong again sounded, calling us to lunch. The repast was spread out under the pergola as we all gathered and took our places. Just as we had all pitched in and diligently worked to gather the harvest, we now attended to this new task at hand. Two hours and several courses later, we trudged back out to finish off the harvest. Fortunately, our hard work in the morning meant that we worked for only a few more hours.

Again, work stopped and we gathered for the afternoon apero. This time, there was no rush to go anywhere and we enjoyed sharing sore back stories and comparing the size of our blisters. As

Andrea Swan with Monique Guezel

we sat around, Joelle drove by with his tractor and cart filled to overflowing with the bounty of our labours. He was on his way to the cave cooperative with another successful harvest. The following evening, the rains arrived and we smiled at our small contribution to Joelle's wine cellar. If you are in Languedoc in October, there are often opportunities to participate in the harvest. Check out the website "Crème de Languedoc" for vineyards looking for help or the local Mairie may know of vignerons needing help.

As you watch people still out harvesting the last of the bounty, you may notice that there are likely no children in the fields unless it is the weekend. In France, the old ways meant that the children were expected to help out with the harvest and therefore, were exempt from a month of school. Over the past decades, this has dwindled down until now there is no exemption—an education is seen as more important than the harvest. This has contributed to the shift from the rural to urban lifestyles that is plaguing France. While not as common in the southern Languedoc, certainly in the rural Cevennes and other remote parts of France, this de-population of the rural communities and farms is changing the face of France. The connection to *terroir* is becoming less a reality and more a myth.

We drove up into the hills on a quiet Sunday afternoon, in search of a vineyard that Monique and Pierre had raved about. We climbed from the lowlands around Beziers up into the foothills of the Montagne Noire with the landscape quickly changing from flat, cultivated vineyards wherever the eye could see to the grey limestone with its scrubby evergreen bushes and cedar and pine trees. The river Orb rushed below us through the rapids created by the narrow canyon walls. We finally found the sign to the winery and turned off onto the winding track road. Before us lay the tiny hamlet of Caza Viel. The tasting room was not opened but the worker who greeted us went in search of the patron. M. Miguel was happy to share his story with us as he poured various bottles of wine for us to taste. The vineyard had been in his family for several centuries and he himself, had given up a career as a banker to follow his passion. However, we learned that the land itself had been first culti-vated by the Romans when retired soldiers were given land throughout the south of France as a way to maintain a presence and keep the peace with the locals. During the twelveth century it was given by Hugues de Cessenon to the Monastery of Fondfroide. The monks made wine for whichthey became renowned. After the Revolution in 1789, the monks were evicted and the land was taken by the state. In 1791 the Miquel family purchased the property but it was primarily used for hunting. It wasn't until 1870 that the first vines were planted and winemak-ing began again. Nine generations of Miquels have worked this land and are now producing

Andrea Swan with Monique Guezel

award-winning wines. As he poured, M Miquel described where the grapes came from, the method used to create the wine—only a single filtration to ensure that all the goodness of the wine remained and the families' commitment to producing quality wines. The Viognier wine was excellent and he explained how the grape variety had moved from northeastern France to the Galacia region of Spain and from there, he introduced it to his small plot in Languedoc. He emphasized how each terroir would change the grape, producing a uniqueness reflective of the sun and soil. As we sipped the wine during the presentation, we could sense the warmth and richness of the hillsides of this small valley. He invited us to return for a full *degustation* (wine tasting). We plan to do so next time, as I'm sure there will be a next time, to search out this delectable find.

Each time we drive through Languedoc, we are amazed to discover yet another hidden gem. The colourful patchwork of the reddening vines, the deep green of the umbrella pines, the rich blue of the cloudless sky and the sharp grey contrast of the jagged stone hills provide an image worthy of the artist's brush.

∞

In France, most festivals and fetes mark the cyclical changes of the year and the impact of those changes on the wellbeing and prosperity of the community. October has several milestones celebrating the ripening, maturing and harvesting of a variety of foods. Pigs, olives, chestnuts, hazelnuts and wine are the five products of Languedoc that have special festivals honouring their contributions to life in the south. The festival of the pig celebrates the end of an abundant summer. In Languedoc, most farms are small plots of stony, terroir that cannot sustain large herds of animals. Most land is scrubland where the animals must be able to forage themselves. This means that pigs, sheep and goats do better than cows in this harsh environment. Sheep and goats were not eaten because they guaranteed an ongoing supply of milk and cheese for several years. Pigs were the main meat source because they grew to maturity in a season and all parts of them could be preserved, cured or salted in some way to ensure an ongoing supply of meat throughout the cold winter months. Particularly, in the mountainous High Languedoc areas such as Lozere, the Cevennes and the Causse, life has traditionally been hard in winter and care must be taken to ensure an adequate supply of food. Many of the customs are no longer needed with the advent of freezers, supermarkets and prepared foods. However, there is still a strong practice of food preservation and food security. After all, this is a country that is only sixty years from knowing the hardships of famine. Memories are justifiably strong and skills are preserved and honoured. By including visits into the haute Languedoc in an October travel itinerary, there is a good chance of happening upon many of the festivals in this region.

Chestnuts and walnuts were dietary staples in the haute Languedoc. The nuts were milled into flour and were used as the main carbohydrate source for daily breads and cakes. Several festivals still celebrate this annual harvest.

> When the leaves have fallen from the vines in the southern Languedoc regions, we know that it is time to head up into the hills to see the changing colours of the leaves of the large deciduous trees of the northern region. We also know that the walnut and chestnut harvest is finishing and celebrations are beginning. The weekend festival in St. Pons de Thomieres is an annual event that features chestnut and walnut delicacies and is the showcase for all regional, fall goodies. We were treated to presentations of medieval singers, dancers and fighters, workshops on preparing traditional foods of the region and of course, samples of delectable fare such as roasting chestnuts. While the festival has taken on a decidedly modern, touristy feeling, the themes, foods and presentations all hark back to a peek into life of an earlier, much more difficult era. It is hard to escape this reality anywhere in Languedoc, which is probably the reason that many are drawn to the region.

There is another harvest taking place in Languedoc this month and that is the olive harvest. Olives for eating will be harvested in October while those for pressing into olive oil will wait until November and December, depending on the variety. While it is well known for new and improving wines, Languedoc is justly famous for fine olive varieties. Like the vines, the olive trees were established here by the Greeks and Romans. There are several particular varieties that thrive here: picholine, Lucque, negrette, rougette, verdale, bouteillan and aglandeau. The picholine and Lucques are excellent for eating. There are numerous mills located throughout Languedoc and like vineyards, they typically offer tours, tastings and a wide variety of product. Moulin de Mont Ramus is located near Pezenas and is now our favourite place for exceptional, local oils. The olives come from either their own groves or two nearby *oliviers* (olive farms).

∞

October is a perfect month to focus on the culinary treasures of Languedoc. While it certainly celebrates the traditional foods of the region such as cassoulet, cheeses, seafood dishes and hearty stews, there is an emerging desire by young chefs to create lighter, more imaginative dishes that reflect a wider range of the produce of the region. These young chefs are not located in the major centers of the region but typically are hidden in out-of-the-way villages, hamlets and countryside. Their reputation is being spread by word of mouth like some secret code to be shared among friends. Whether you prefer the traditional foods of Languedoc or want to discover these new gastronomic stars, be prepared to appreciate not only the dishes but the settings, the ambiance and the prices for these experiences.

The settings are invariably wonderful. Old stone auberges have huge walk-in fireplaces and rooms for the night. Abandoned church houses perch high on the gorge below. Tiny, hole-in-the-wall niches are tucked in between other larger buildings. Low buildings slump alongside the Canal du Midi where the passing barges offer an ever-changing panorama to set the scene. Small, intimate places off the beaten track, high up in the Cevennes where the journey to reach them is part of the experience. The ambiance of each restaurant is unique but, in our experience, there have been consistent hallmarks of each one: the presentation of the meals has shown what pride the chefs take in preparing the food and showing it off to its best advantage, the small, additional treats of an *amuse bouche* (palate teaser) that typically link each course are unique and presented as un petit cadeau to encourage you to pace yourself, savour the dishes and understand that you are their guest—there is no expectation to hurry away. It has been said that in good restaurants in France, there is no second service—the customer essentially has rented the table for the duration of the lunch or dinner so the customer can take time in order to appreciate all the work that the chef has done to prepare the meal. Connections are commonly made with the other guests as these restaurants are often small with few tables so diners acknowledge each other with *bon appétit or bonne continuation* (bonne continuation will be said as main courses are being presented) and conversations strike up easily. The chef and his helper, who is often his partner, come and greet each guest to make sure that the meal is pleasing. It becomes quickly apparent that many of the guests have become good friends as well as good customers.

The major surprise continues to be how reasonably priced these wonderful meals are. In the off season such as October, the restaurants are still open but may have reduced hours on Sunday evening and be closed on Monday and Tuesday. Sunday lunch is usually open as this is the traditional day for *en famille* (family) dining. Long, lunches lasting well into the late afternoon where family members of all ages gather to savour the food and share the news of the week. The prices range from 20 euros for a three course meal up to 55-60 euros for the chef's special multi course meal. Of course, this price includes taxes and tips.

It was a special occasion with good friends and we had recently heard about Le Presbytre in Vailhan. The local reviews were good so we headed out on a bright Sunday morning. The map suggested that it was only 20 minutes away but Mr. GPS had obviously never driven the road! After leaving the larger towns behind, we headed up into the hills, travelling along increasingly narrow roads until it seemed we were on cart tracks. Could this be correct? Then suddenly, signposts guided us forward. "Bon Courage" as Monique would say and we persevered on. By now, all signs of civilization had disappeared but as we turned the next hairpin corner before us lay a small lake and perched atop the hillside that overlooked the lake was a medieval sandstone building. As M. GPS says, "you have reached your destination." L'Auberge de Presbtere is a tiny restaurant with a huge heart and imagination. Because it is an auberge, there is accommodation on site. Any establishment with "Auberge" in the name means that it offers accommodation which is a good thing to know if one is heading out for a late gourmet meal with a variety of wines. The young chef, Baptiste and his wife, Martine have room for seven tables inside as well as a small terrace for summer dining. The view is spectacular if one can tear their eyes away from the food presentations to check it out. As Martine presents the first course, she wishes us "bon appetit" and when the second course arrived, she said "bonne continuation". Martine shared her extensive knowledge of the local wines by explaining where each one came from and the characteristics produced by the soil and growing conditions. Baptiste made an appearance from the kitchen late in the meal to receive customers' reactions to his cooking. We were *à table* (sitting and eating) for four hours, enjoying the food, the company and the scenery.

Young chefs such as Baptiste are popping up all over Languedoc. In our area alone, a few hidden gems include O Bontemps in Magalas, L'Auberge de la Croisade, Auberge des Combes, Auberge des Causses and Restaurant Lou Regalou. Part of the joys of October is discovering each of them and adding to the growing list to share with friends and family.

∞

In considering the stories of the chefs and their families, there is a thread that runs through each one. That is the passion and dedication they bring to food, preparation and service.

Monique and I discussed this recently as we prepared the dishes for October. As we visit restaurants in the slower pace of October, I am struck how these young chefs are forgoing the fame and fortune of the big cities to focus on a more deliberate vocation of creating imaginative, careful meals that mirror the landscape and the producers who support them. She replied that many of them are returning to their roots and that they have often learned their love of cooking and using good produce at the knees of grandmère and from working the terroir of grandpère's farm.

∞

It was a warm, sunny, autumn afternoon when Monique and I prepared these three recipes. Typically, she directs me in helping to prepare ingredients à la française; I write frantically, trying to translate her French gestures into cooking terms and we *rigolons* (laugh & have fun) over the joys of cooking. Even with all this, we put together these three courses in under one hour.

SAUTÉ DE PORC

Monique says that this recipe is often used as an excuse for using up all the bits of vegetables lying around. As we prepared the dish, she asked for bits of this and that. Fortunately, as this is an autumn dish, we had the last potatoes, carrots and onions that we had just harvested. The amounts mentioned below easily provide a hearty meal for 4-6 people. If you plan on serving it for several meals, only cook enough potatoes for each meal as, according to Monique, cooked potatoes become tough when refrigerated.

Ingredients for 6 persons:

2 Tablespoons oil

2 ½ lbs pork shoulder should cut into 2 inch cubes

3-4 carrots sliced into 2 inch lengths

2 diced onions

1 cut up celery branch with leaves

5-6 potatoes

1 small can sliced mushrooms and reserve the liquid

½ can whole, pitted green olives without the brine

1 cup diced canned tomatoes-you can use fresh diced, skinless tomatoes if you have them on hand. An easy trick for skinning tomatoes for this recipe is to cut them in half and grate the raw side using a coarse grater. Be careful as you near the skin that fingers don't get caught on the grater—not appetizing!

Salt and pepper to taste. Watching Monique add salt and pepper is a bit unnerving for careful cooks who like to follow directions. *En principe*, the cook tastes and decides, adding anywhere from a few grains to a heaping teaspoon.

Preparation:

In a large heavy *cocotte*, (Dutch oven or stew pot), add oil and meat. Cook over medium high heat until meat is seared and golden on the edges.

Add the onions, carrots, celery and enough potatoes for this meal. Continue stirring until everything is mixed together. After 5-10 minutes, add the mushrooms, olives, tomatoes and enough water and the mushroom juice to cover everything. Let simmer until meat is tender. It will separate easily when pierced with a fork. Our recipe took about 40 minutes to be tender. When ready, taste the broth and season with salt and pepper as needed.

Serve with fresh bread and a robust red wine.

VELOUTÉ DE POTIMIRON

Potimiron is a deep orange, thick skinned squash found in France. In America it is called Baby Red Hubbarb or Red Kiri squash. Other squashes such as pumpkin could be used but the Potimiron does have a rich nutty taste that adds flavour to the recipe. It is a soup ideally suited to the still warm evenings of Languedoc when heavy evening meals are not the rule.

Ingredients for 4 persons:

2 cups cubed squash, rind removed

1 large potato, cubed

½ cup low fat milk

1 chicken cube plus 2 cups water or 2
cups prepared chicken broth

3-5 tablespoons creme fraiche

Salt and pepper to taste

¼ cup chopped parsley

Preparation:

Put squash, potato, milk, parsley and chicken cube and water or broth into a large, heavy saucepan and cook on medium heat. Bring to a boil and reduce heat to a simmer until the vegetables are well cooked and soft. Strain off the liquid and set it aside.

Purée vegetable mixture until creamy, adding enough of the liquid to produce a thick soup. Add salt & pepper to taste. Add 3 tablespoons crème fraiche just before serving. If you prefer a richer flavour add the five tablespoons of crème fraiche and forget the calories.

This soup re-heats well if there is any left. Serve with fresh baguette and a cheese & fruit plate for a complete evening meal.

TARTE AUX POMMES

The beauty of this dessert is that it is so simple to make, so classically French and makes you look like an artist. What more can you ask for?

Ingredients:

Prepared pastry such as a pie crust
dough rolled into a 12 inch circle

2 large apples-the French typically use
Golden Delicious in cooking

½ cup applesauce-homemade or canned

Sugar for sprinkling on tarte

Optional- chopped fresh rosemary leaves

Preparation:

Roll out pastry dough and lay over a sheet of baking paper in a
12 inch round pan

Cover piecrust with a moderately thick layer of applesauce

Quarter apples and slice thinly and evenly.

Lay the apple slices in an overlapping spiral pattern beginning
from the outside edge of the pan and working towards the
middle until all the piecrust is covered. For an interesting variation, a friend added chopped fresh rosemary leaves to the top of
the apples after layering them in the piecrust.

Sprinkle the apples with a light coat of sugar

Bake in 375°F oven and check after 20 minutes. Bake until
golden brown. Remove from pie tin when cool. Serve warm with
Battu, ice cream, whipping cream, crème fraiche or on its own.

Andrea Swan with Monique Guezel

NOVEMBER

*Feast days, winter storms, remembering,
musical celebrations, bells & whistles*

The grape leaves are slowing turning yellow and scattering the ground; the early morning air is nippy as one hustles to the boulangerie for baquettes & croissants; scarves and puffy coats are the appearing—at least until mid-morning when the sun has burned off the morning mist and people start donning sunglasses. There is tranquility to village life as it's the time between the end of the grape harvest and the beginning of the Christmas season. There are few visitors around and for someone who wants to practice their French language skills, November offers plenty of opportunities. November in Languedoc would appeal to those who enjoy quiet times immersing themselves in a community. The feast days, the cultural events and the sounds and smells of the French countryside make November a unique time to visit.

As the weather marks the changing seasons, so too do the feast days that bookend November. The month begins on a somber note with Toussaint (All Saints) and the tributes to the dead and ends with the celebrations of the Feast of St. Cecilia, the patron saint of music and the Feast of St. Catherine, the patron saint of successful planting. November offers visitors the chance to participate in significant rituals of the community that have deep roots and great meaning.

∞

If you arrive in Languedoc at the end of October, you may wonder why chrysanthemums in a multitude of colours appear to be the only flowers in the shops, or are the preferred floral arrangements adorning the Mairie flowerboxes or on balconies throughout the region. According to legend, the chrysanthemum represents happiness and eternity and is therefore, the plant used to commemorate the Nov.1st, All Saints' Day. Up until the eighth century, Nov 1st had been the time of pagan rituals marking the "dark half of the year" and the period of death and decay. In the eighth century, Pope Gregory decreed that Catholics would now give homage to all the saints who had died. As with many Catholic traditions, this was an attempt to integrate Catholicism into the preexisting rituals and beliefs.

Andrea Swan with Monique Guezel

Officially, Nov. 2nd is All Souls Day, the day designated for families to honour their dead. Frequently the ceremonies are now combined into one ceremony. On Nov.1st, following morning mass at the local church, the priest leads a procession to the cemetery where pots of chrysanthemums are laid on gravesites. Families tend the gravesites and offer prayers and condolences for their dead. The day ends with a family gathering to fondly remember their deceased relatives.

This early November day was perfect for a walk around the village. We turned the corner of the high wall and found ourselves facing an open gate leading into the normally closed graveyard. Laid out in neat rows before us, a central grassed pathway led to the large mausoleum situated against the back wall. The headstones ranged from newly carved stones to old, moss covered ones in the far corner. The writing on the stones told of loss, tragedy, war, pestilence and hardship. Dotted amongst the grey and black, the vivid colours of the chrysanthemums provided a sense of hope and remembrance. Today was Nov. 2nd and the homage had just taken place.

The Famille Morez listed the names of six children aging from 2-9 who died over a period of five years during the time that Spaniards fled to France during the 1936 civil war. The internment of the Spaniards in camps in the southern Languedoc meant incredible hardship and loss. For the Famille Morez, their story on this tombstone speaks volumes and is a reminder of other stories of war and persecution.

The Famille Esteve listed names back to 1740 in an unbroken line of members who stayed in the village and grew in both numbers and fame with buildings and streets denoting their importance. The names and dates of their birth and death show a hardy family, long-lived and prosperous. Even today, the patron of our village is a member of the Esteve family whose roots date back to medieval times.

We turned into the far corner and there in front of me was a prominent headstone with my family name boldly inscribed. This was a surprising find as my French ancestors came from Normandie in the fifteenth century during the Huguenot persecutions. I did not realize that some had established in Languedoc. Somehow being in the graveyard on Nov. 2nd amid stories of both persecution and resilience seemed right as I remembered my own family history and those who are no longer with me.

All Hallows Eve (Halloween) was not celebrated in France the way it is in North America. However, there is a creeping influence beginning with the appearance of children's costumes and candy. If you see a leftover witch on a broomstick plastered to a wall or telephone pole, you can be certain that North American Halloween customs have come to the village.

Andrea Swan with Monique Guezel

∞

As November creeps along, the "dark half of the year" begins even in Languedoc. The days are getting shorter and any rain is likely to happen in the first weeks of this month. While not persistent over days, as in October, rain in November tends to fall heavily over a short period of time. The creeks and rivers swell rapidly as the parched summer earth drains off the water. This means that attention must be paid to where you park your car or where you wander off in the hills.

> The pounding on the door at 3AM was terrifying especially as the words being yelled at us were in French and obviously urgent. "*La voiture, la voiture*" yelled Monique, banging vigourously on our door, "*inondation, inondation*" (flooding, flooding) as my husband scrambled to find his clothes. Racing down the hill to the floodway where we had parked the car securely for the night, we were greeted with the Pompiers (Fire brigade) who had closed off the road due to the rapidly swelling streambed. Within minutes, the rain water had come hurdling down from the mountains north of us, increasing in velocity as tributaries along the way emptied their deluge until now, close to the mouth of the river, the creek had risen several feet entrapping cars parked on the banks. By the time my husband managed to get the car running, the water was filling the floor and wetting the mats. Other car owners were not

so lucky and tow trucks were rapidly deployed to haul away cars to higher ground. Fortunately, the crisis passed quickly and by morning the streambed was back to its mild meandering course. However, it was a good lesson on November storms and a cautionary tale of parking perils. The next day Monique alerted us to the change in weather—strong winds from the north would now arrive and chase away the moisture filled clouds leaving us with barren vines and cold, clear sunny skies. November weather is a dramatic mix of conditions that mark the transition from growth and harvest to rest and renewal.

∞

In most areas of rural France, firefighting is carried out by a highly trained group of local volunteers. They are called SapeurPompiers as a remnant of war where the sapeurs would dig trenches and underground tunnels and the pompiers fought fires. These men and women respond quickly and effectively to a wide range of emergencies from rescuing a beloved cat in a tree to attending medical emergencies and extinguishing blazes. In return, November is the time when they request the communities' support to maintain their services.

Phillipe arrived at the door late one November evening offering a copy of the annual calendar, the sale of which funds many of the Sapeur Pompier volunteer activities such as supporting the fire cadets in their training. Fortunately, we

Andrea Swan with Monique Guezel

had been alerted to this practice and were prepared with our donation for the calendar. After
a chat about the weather and how his visits
were going, he proceeded on his way for his late
evening dinner. Having watched the team in
action, the price of the calendar seemed a small
cost for the security of having such a committed
group so close at hand.

∞

Nowhere is there greater understanding of the horror of
the Great War, the "war to end all wars", than in France where
the loss of life and the abominable conditions of war were felt
so heavily by so many countries. The monument in the Place
du Commemeration is a reminder how many young men
of the village lost their lives in this way. Being in Languedoc
in November offers the chance to participate in the Armistice
ceremonies and deepen one's understanding of the reality of
giving up one's youth for a cause and also reminds visitors of
how life existed under the conditions of war.

The men were old and bent as they walked
slowly in formation from the church to the
cenotaph to mark the November 11th ceremonies. We had watched the ceremonies for the
past few years and noted that each year, fewer
men participated. And experiences of the Great
war lived only in the memories of this elderly
people. These elderly people were the last living
reminders of the Second World War. The tall,

young mayor strode proudly at the head of the line, resplendent in his sash of office. Only he, with the broad smile on his face, seemed to miss the gravity of the event so clearly etched on the faces of the old men and women. The local high school students began their presentation in halting English and I quickly realized that they were reciting our Canadian emblem of Armistice ceremonies—In Flanders Fields, written so long ago by the Canadian surgeon, John McRae during his time in Flanders. After they spoke, I gave my own Canadian symbol, my *coquelicot*, (poppy), to the young student in appreciation for her efforts. In France, the floral symbol is not the poppy but the *bluet* (blue cornflower) that also marked the graves of those young men. Languedoc lived under war conditions of rationing and deprivation during WWI and under occupation during WWII. According to our German neighbours, this is the day that they tend to stay home as hard feelings and difficult memories still linger. The music and the messages are somber and recall the roll that the village played for La France. After everyone joins in singing the national anthem, La Marseillaise, people drift over to the Salle de Fetes to share the memories and stories of the war—memories that will soon be lost to current generations. This gathering is not only for the villagers but also for those visitors who want to share in the life of the

Andrea Swan with Monique Guezel

village, not only the good times but also the difficult times.

∞

The feast of St. Cecilia on November 22 is marked by music and concerts throughout Languedoc. This first century Roman saint was known as a patron of the early Christian church musicians. Today, her name is commemorated through the choirs and concerts that focus primarily on religious music. Even though France is officially a secular country, the presence of historical churches provides wonderful concert venues.

The choice was difficult—join a village French choir or a neighbouring English choir. In the end, my husband decided to try both. They proved to be different in style and musical repertoire but both were committed to rigorous practice in preparation for the concerts for St. Cecilia. Both concerts would take place in local churches, one in the village and the other in a distant town that caters to the burgeoning English expatriate community.

The village concert was a chance to meet old friends and get caught up on the local news. Bundled up in our coats, scarves and gloves, we huddled in the main section of the old village church trying to get as close as possible to the few portable heaters. The choir members were all well known to the audience and waves and head nods signaled their arrival. However, once the music began, there was rapt attention paid to the singers. Their song choices included a number of different languages and musical complexity for such a small amateur choir. Their enthusiasm and dedication showed in the caliber of the singing. Of course, the evening ended with a verre d'amitie and more conversation.

The concert in the other village attracted a different audience and felt more as though we were in some small English village. The British accents murmuring around us made us forget that we were in the heart of Languedoc. The repertoire was lovely and carried us back to memories of well-loved English hymns. The food selection at the end was mince tarts and wine! Regardless of the choirs, the chance to attend a wide variety of musical events is a highlight of late November in Languedoc.

∞

Monique quoted, "A la Sainte Catherine, tout bois prend racine" (On the feast of St Catherine's, all trees take root). St. Catherine is another beloved saint in Languedoc as she is believed to watch over the planting of trees to ensure their successful survival. Although, tree growers reassure us that anytime during this dormant period is a good time to plant, there is still a strong belief in these wise words from long ago.

Andrea Swan with Monique Guezel

From the masses of chrysanthemums in late October to the multitude of young trees, the Saturday flower market's array of colours and variety makes it a "go to" stall. We had checked our small garden area thoroughly and figured we knew what kind of small tree would work. After intense questioning by the *pepiniere* (fruit tree seller), he decided that we couldn't possibly plant such a tree in our garden conditions. Instead, he provided excellent advice and on November 25th, under sunny skies, we carefully planted our new tree in the garden, silently invoking St. Catherine to watch over it. Over the year, the white blossoms herald spring, the thick branches guard us from the hot summer sun and provides cooling shade and in November, the glossy green leaves are the only remnants of a fading year.

Monique explained that while the celebration of St. Catherine as the patron saint of plants taking root continues today, St. Catherine was also the patron saint of unmarried women. Traditionally, women over the age of twenty-five who had not yet found a husband, wore a white cap on her head. In this day and age, there would be sea of white caps doting the streetscape. Fortunately, times change and some traditions die out although the advent of matchmaking websites suggests that old traditions don't die out, they simply change to modern conditions.

∞

With the tourists now gone, the grape harvesting machines now silent and the cooler weather keeping windows closed, November offers the chance for other sounds to be clearly heard. Before the telephone and Internet, most French villages used loudspeakers and klaxons to alert residents to both emergencies and opportunities. Today, the siren calls the volunteer fire brigade and the loudspeaker announces the arrival of the bread truck, the fisherman and the butcher.

> The first time we heard the high pitched siren, we wondered what had happened; was there a national emergency; was this an air raid siren; was there something we were supposed to do. Monique said that this siren alerted the fire brigade to rush to the *caserne* (firehall) and prepare for an emergency. We also learned that every Wednesday at noon, a practice siren rings out to ensure that all systems are working. As I listen to the siren calling the volunteers, I realize that there is another sound immediately following the alarm—the baying of all the local hunting dogs responding to the call and the neighbours' rooster joining the chorus.
>
> It was a warm sunny morning when we bicycled to the small, neighbouring village. As we sat in the sunshine outside the bar, we heard a loudspeaker blaring out "le pecheur de Valras arrive" (the fisherman from Valras has arrived). We

watched as doors opened and women hurried out with their shopping baskets to the centre of the village in order to have the pick of the best fish. This would mean that Thursday is fish day in most of the village homes. We arrived as the serious cooks of the village were completing their purchases. Coming from a country with more limited choice, we were bewildered by the array of whole fish staring back at us on the iced trays in the van. M Le Pecheur quickly understood our dilemma and asked us a series of questions to help us decide on our purchase. The preparation and serving of the dish was as important as the purchase and our satisfaction in having a "bon repas" was as important to him as the fish we bought. Throughout Languedoc, we have continually encountered this attention to the finer points of the meal and appreciation of the food. As Monique says, it is important to honour the food source and the people who have provided it by taking care in the preparation and the serving of a meal. Following our fish purchase, we next stood in line, carefully picking out fruit and vegetables to accompany the meal. As we waited for our turn to pay Bernadette, our items nestled in the familiar green basket, we were surrounded by older women chatting in French and laughing among themselves. As the laughter rose, we realized what they were talking about. One elderly woman was reminding her neighbour who appeared to be well into her 80s that she would need to be careful about feeding her husband all that celery she had in her green basket because after all, as everyone knew, celery is a strong aphrodisiac and she might be needing her copy of the Kama Sutra! When they realized that I understood the conversation, we were included in the group and the woman being teased whispered to me that she would need the intervention of the holy spirit if anything was going to happen. Amid continued laughing and joking, we completed our purchases and wished one and all "Bonne journee" and then with a laugh "bonne nuit" (good night). For anyone who wants to practice their French, these everyday opportunities in the quiet of November provide wonderful memories.

The following week, we were up early to take friends to the first train to Paris. After dropping them off at 6:30AM, we made our way over to the Friday morning market in Beziers. This market is clearly for the locals with all manner of clothing, household items and foods to cater to the largely Arab population of this quartier of Beziers. It is a favourite market of ours because of the fresh produce, unusual items and raucous sounds, reminiscent of visits to North Africa. This morning, however, was different. The merchants were just setting up in the darkness of the November morning. There was an eerie quietness as the merchants busily set up their stalls in the dim, cold light. As one of the first people to arrive at the stands, we

Andrea Swan with Monique Guezel

felt like intruders, arriving before our hosts were ready to receive us. We made our way to the local brasserie on the corner, out of the chill of the early morning air. Inside was like a neighbourhood Paris bistro where all the locals had gathered. All the customers were greeted with a bisous (except us) and a café. It was quickly apparent that the patron knew all the regulars and their menu choices as decisions were made with the quick nod of the head in understanding. Coffee and a pastry were quickly devoured as people headed back out into the frosty air to tend their stands. By the time we returned, the atmosphere had changed completely with morning light was entering the Place du Marché; les grandmères were pushing their carts in search of the best produce and meats, out early to beat the crowds; and, refreshed from their cafe fix, the merchants were beginning the cacophony of sound that heralds the arrival of this normal market experience.

∞

France is officially a secular country with a clear distinction between church and state. However, the Catholic Church remains a strong identifying feature of French life. While the people attending church are typically old, white-haired women, the churches themselves are clear reminders of a more relevant past. No village is too small to not have at least one church or chapel. In times past, they were the centre of village life, marking the hours, days and months of the year. While they continue to mark daily life as their bells sound out the half and full hours of the day, it is in the quiet of November when these bells can most clearly be heard.

The small, perched village was nestled in the pass of two mountain ranges in the Pyrenées foothills. Isolated from neighbours except for the winding road, the sounds of daily life were remarkable because of the sounds reverberating off the hillsides. We had arrived late the previous night and immediately fell into a deep sleep. In the early morning, well before we anticipated being up, our sleep was broken by the loud peeling of bells. A quick look at our clock revealed 6AM! We quickly realized that this was not going to stop and that there was a pattern to the ringing: one peel indicated fifteen minutes past the hour; three intermittent peels meant the half hour and the hour chime rang twice—once on the hour and again about 5 minutes later again, indicating the hour—in this case, 6 peels of the bell. Monique's explanation for this was to ensure that in case anyone missed the first hourly bell, they would hear the second chime. She also explained that until quite recently, the bells had rung out during the night as well but the villagers had petitioned the Mairie to have the practice stopped. After several months and numerous discussions, the Church had been instructed to ring the bells only from 6AM to 11PM.

We did get used to the early bells and as we started our vacation in the village, we soon listened for the sounds that began to govern our

Andrea Swan with Monique Guezel

day: the 8AM bells meant that cars and children's voices would soon be heard as people headed out to work and school; the 10AM bell was the time for *le pause*, time to head to the café for a morning coffee and a chat with friends or a quiet read of the newspaper; noon bells alerted us that the village would become quiet as villagers headed inside for the main meal of the day; the 4PM bell was time for goutée and for children to have their afternoon snack (and adults too); 6PM was time to head for home as the darkness of the night descended on the village and finally, the 9PM bells meant that all good children should be home in bed. This slower-paced timekeeping allowed us to put away our watches and settle into a rhythm attuned more to the life, the seasons and our stomachs!

∞

The market was crowded with locals on the day I decided to make Monique's Boeuf Bourguigon. I approached the butcher's stall and indicated that I wanted to make Boeuf Bourguignon and could he tell me what cut of meat I should use. Leaning over from the next stall, the *fromagerie* (cheese seller) wanted to know how many people were coming and when I would be serving the dish. I said 6 people were coming the next evening for dinner. His response was, what time are you serving dinner? I wasn't sure if he was looking for an invitation or preparing a detailed recipe for me to follow. The woman at the egg stall on the other side of the butcher leaned in and wanted to know what wine I would be using in the recipe as only a Pinot Noir was the proper wine to use. Between the three of them, they decided on the cut, the amount of meat, the cooking time and the accompaniments for the dish. Not only did I prepare a wonderful Boeuf Bourguignon using Monique's recipe but I have wonderful memories of the purchase. Perhaps, you can have your own wonderful memories.

BOEUF BOURGUIGNON
À LA MONIQUE

Ingredients for 6 people:

¼ cup cooking oil

1 ½ kg (3 lbs) beef cut into large cubes (tell the butcher that you want to make an excellent boeuf bourguignon and ask him to give you the correct cuts)

6-8 pieces pork rind (not likely sold at the local supermarket-talk to your butcher)

3 medium carrots cut in thin coins

1 cooking onion chopped into small pieces

3 cloves crushed garlic *en chemise* (unpeeled)

4 sprigs of fresh thyme or 1 teaspoon dried

1 bay leaf

1 tablespoon flour

Salt & pepper to taste

⅔ bottle of good red wine. Monique says that a good cook uses the same wine in a recipe as will be served with the meal. In this case, a Merlot works well.

Preparation:

Place oil in heavy casserole pot on medium high heat. Add beef and keep turning to brown on all sides.

Once meat is browned, add chopped onion, carrots and pork rind.

Crush the garlic gloves using the broad side of a large knife then add to meat mixture.

Add ¼ teaspoon each salt and pepper, thyme and bay leaf

Sprinkle flour over meat

In a separate saucepan, bring the wine to a low boil for several minutes to allow some of the alcohol to burn off. According to Monique, this will prevent the meat from toughening. After wine has simmered, add to meat mixture along with enough water to cover.

Leave mixture to boil gently for "un bon moment" (1-½ hrs) checking regularly to ensure that meat is covered with liquid. Add water as needed.

After "un bon moment", check that the meat is tender by inserting a knife-texture should be similar to a cooked cake as it slides in with little resistance.

Once the meat is tender, move pot to *un coin au feu*. Monique explains how her grandmère would now move the casserole to the edge of the open hearth of the fireplace to allow the casserole to slowly cook over many hours. You can do the same with a low oven temperature or a wood stove if you have one. Remove the pork rind before serving. Adjust salt and pepper seasoning.

Serve with broad noodles or potatoes, salad and lots of baguette and the same red wine used in cooking. This dish is perfect for the windy, rainy nights of early November and if there is any left over, add some barley for a wonderful hearty soup.

I have been fascinated by the assortment of prepared pastry crusts available in the dairy cases in any supermarket or *épicerie* (small grocery store) throughout France. They range from *pate feuilletée* (puff pastry) to *pate sableé* (similar to a shortbread crust) and *pate brisé* (pie crust). They come in single packages ready to unroll into a 14" round. They even come wrapped in their own parchment paper so you can easily lay them directly on a baking sheet.

Early in our education into French life, Monique explained that the main dinner meal is typically eaten at lunchtime with a smaller, lighter meal at night. This helps the *le digestion* and makes it easier to sleep.

She has chosen two tarte *salées* (savoury) recipes for November as they are both often featured this month. Served with a salad, they make a wonderfully light evening meal.

TARTE AUX ENDIVES

Ingredients:

2 packages puff pastry or enough for
the top and bottom of the tarte

2-4 Belgian Endives

300 grams chèvre (goat cheese)

1 package of lardons or 6 strips of bacon

Salt and pepper to taste

1 egg beaten

Small piece of aluminum foil

Preparation:

Cut each endive in half widthwise and peel apart all the leaves

With a bit of olive oil in the pan, lightly sauté the sections until they are soft

Sauté the lardons or bacon strips until crisp-crumble bacon when done

Place pastry into baking dish and pierce with a fork

Place the endive sections onto pastry and cover with lardons

Cut the chèvre into thin rounds and layer over the pastry, endives and lardons

Cover with remaining pastry and pierce the crust lightly,

Brush crust lightly with beaten egg

Roll the piece of aluminum foil, pierce the top pasty crust and make a small chimney in the centre of the crust.

Place in oven at 350°F and after 20 minutes, as Monique says 'keep an eye on the oven". Tart should be golden brown and puffy when finished.

As with all the recipes, Monique prepares and cooks them as I translate the ingredients and techniques into English. In this case, when it came time to brush the pastry with the beaten egg, we realized that we did not have a pastry brush. "Pas de problème" says Monique and quickly takes a fork and wraps a bit of paper toweling around it. Voila, a pastry brush!

TARTE AUX POIREAUX (LEEKS)

Ingredients:

1 package of puff pastry

2 leeks with significant white stems, otherwise, 3 leeks

3 eggs

½ cup crème fraiche

1 package lardons (use thick bacon chopped into small pieces)

1 onion, chopped

½ cup shredded Gruyere cheese

Salt & pepper to taste

Oil for sautéing leeks

Preparation:

Chop the white ends of the leeks into thin rounds. Sauté for several minutes then add onion and bacon, mixing well. Sauté until all are soft-approximately 7-10 minutes. Remove from heat and let cool.

Roll out the pastry into a round 14" pan. Pierce the bottom several times with a fork.

In a bowl, mix together the eggs, salt & pepper, crème fraiche. Add to the cooled leek and onion mixture.

Add mixture to pastry and sprinkle with grated cheese.

Bake at 350°F for 30 minutes. Serve hot with a fresh salad.

DECEMBER

walkabouts, les Halles, Circulade
towns, Christmas traditions

December in France seems like two distinct times: the first half carries on much as November with the sunny, warm days shortening as winter approaches, enjoying the opportunities to be quietly immersed in the culture and living the French experience. By mid-December the tempo changes as thoughts, decorations and advertising remind us that Christmas will soon be here. Christmas in France is about family, Père Noel, special foods, music and celebrations. Unlike in North America, the frantic Christmas shopping season is much shorter and more muted, focusing on preparing lavish dinners for family and showering young children with gifts.

Being in Languedoc in December offers the chance to participate in local festivities and experience the extensive array of foods, markets and traditions of the Christmas season. But it also offers the chance to explore the rituals that underpin these cultural events.

> At the tabac, we saw the notice for the walk to visit the crosses of the village sponsored by the local Arts et Culture Association. We signed up and met the group at the appointed time. As with many local villages, there are active groups who organize a wide range of activities for anyone to participate in. Some are courses that continue for a few weeks but many are single events that are well worth the cost because it is a chance to meet people, learn more about the culture and the village and have a fun time. This event was billed as a free, two-hour walk around the village following the green route noted in the local handbook of self-guided walking tours of the village.
>
> Monsieur Gaudin was the local historian and guide for the walk and as such had researched the many crosses that dot the village. Many

of them dated back a few hundred years but others had been "borrowed" and "repurposed" at newer sites. Some denoted local events or tragedies; some were way-markers to suggest pilgrimage routes; and others were mysteries of time past. It was interesting to pass an afternoon trying out our limited French and being encouraged to join in. Inevitably, someone spoke "a little English" and would help us stumble along. We learned some local history; we made new friends; we walked out in the December sunshine among the vineyards and, finally, we ended our day at a local Chateau sharing wine and conversation. This is what life can be like in December in Languedoc, even for a visitor.

∞

Along with the numerous crosses that dot the villages and countryside, there is another religious element that is frequently seen throughout France and especially in the south. While fewer than 30 percent of the French population indicate an adherence to a religion, nonetheless, the Virgin Mary features prominently in life outside the churches themselves. As a clay statue, she peaks out from niches in house walls; as a tall, imposing carved marble figure, she stands guard at village crossroads; as a moss covered wooden totem, she suddenly appears in wooded lanes and as a golden, flaming motif, she sits benignly atop the entrance to the church. She can appear in the most unusual places.

We were wandering through each room of the house that was to become our new home in France. We thought that we had checked out every nook and cranny thoroughly to ensure that this would meet our needs. After much discussion, we knew that it was our *coup de coeur* (spoke to our heart) and we made the purchase. We were now ready to begin the move and prepare to settle in. Another close inspection was in order, this time looking more closely as furniture and other items had been removed by the previous owners. The smallest bedroom had contained several items that had prevented us from checking windows and doors. We had forgotten about the small window overlooking the neighbour's terrace. The latch was stuck and the hinges looked old and rusty. After several tugs and some lubricating oil, the window swung open and much to our surprise was a ceramic bust of the Virgin Mary staring back at us. Her nose was slightly chipped and her blue carved veil now looked pale under a crust of lichen. She looked lost and forgotten in the window but somehow, we felt that she must have sat here for an extended length of time. Who were we to dislodge her from her perch? Instead, we carefully swept off the lichen and burnished her blue veil. Nothing could improve the chip on her nose but better there than on her shoulder!! She continues to live in the windowsill of the small bedroom and perhaps offers comfort to those who visit. We do have one visitor who requests this room and has grown comfortable with her sharing his space.

Whether tucked into a niche in a house or occupying a central position in a village, these statues remind visitors of the centuries-old traditions that permeate the region. Likely remnants of pagan deities, this female goddess of the last two thousand years continues to evoke a need for a female presence in peoples' lives.

∞

Large supermarkets or hypermarchés are springing up all over France but in reality the concept of centralized shopping for all your food needs has been in existence for centuries. *Les Halles*, the large, covered buildings found in all large cities throughout France continue to provide permanent spaces for individual merchants offering all sorts of foods. The buildings are typically marked by their large multiple arches on all four sides opening onto a town square. December offers the chance to visit many of these throughout Languedoc. Toulouse has a large Halles, covering a full city block; Narbonne's is a noisy, bustling place any day of the week; Beziers' is showing signs of aging as commercial life in the *centre ville* (city center) is seeping out into the edges of town and there are rumors that it may close and Sete, located on the coast is a congested mix of numerous seafood and fruit and vegetable merchants. There are a few consistent features of the Halles: there is always good parking nearby to encourage and support the local market; the markets are only open in the morning, usually until 1PM; there are always lots of free samples of various food bits; and regardless of the time, there are always bars busy serving both alcohol and coffee; and each market conveys an energy specific to the locale.

We had just picked up guests from the Toulouse airport and headed into the city center to look around. We quickly found ourselves driving down small, one-way streets and finally dead-ended in front of trucks unloading produce and meat. We were not going anywhere soon so parked the car in the adjacent car park and headed into the unknown. This was our introduction to les Halles Victor Hugo of Toulouse. We quickly became overwhelmed by the number of meat vendors with their specialties hanging from hooks over the counter: cured hams with the hooves still attached so that the knowledgeable buyer could ensure that this ham, indeed, came from a black pig as listed on the sign; cured sausage coils, strings, rounds and slabs all made from every part of the animal. In the front of the case, sat trays of lamb and veal tongues ready to prepare into gellied dishes or tasty ragouts; next were calves brains, hearts, livers and stomachs all displayed for the discerning cook. Our first reaction was needless to say, a bit of a shock. North Americans are used to seeing their meat in nice, sanitary Styrofoam packages with little evidence of the original size or shape of the animal part. The fowl counters were a picture from an old painting with each bird hanging by its beak from a large hook over the counter. Feathers and feet of ducks, guinea fowl, chicken, quail, and geese were still attached and except for the glazed eyes, it was difficult to realize that the birds were dead and not stuffed by a local taxidermist. The counter that finally did in our young guests was the one the read "Chevaline". Our two young horse enthusiasts were horrified as they slowly used their school French to decipher the handpainted sign. Could it really be?! Yes, most definitely, horsemeat is a common red meat in French diets. We quickly passed by the other chevaline stalls as we made our way to the bread and pastry area. The aroma of fresh bread is always a strong draw and this was no exception. The quality was excellent and the numerous samples kept us well fed.

Narbonne on a cool December Sunday is an interesting experience. Only the locals are around and shoppers are serious as items are bought for Sunday dinner. The Narbonnais may have a sweeter tooth than the Toulousians as there were many more bakery and pastry stalls at the Narbonne Halles. The specialties we found were the *sablées*, large, flat shortbread cookies baked in the shape of the Catalan cross. These were more popular than the flaky pastry cookie called *oreilletes* that were covered with sugar and

Andrea Swan with Monique Guezel

grated orange rind. The best part of these stalls are all the free samples.

The number of flower stalls was impressive not only for their range of bouquets and colours but for the originality of the displays and the prices that seemed so much less than in North America.

Like an older woman trying to compete with the young fashionable girl, the Beziers Halles can be best appreciated by understanding the transformation that is happening in the centre ville. New *centres commercials* (shopping malls) are opening up on the outskirts of Beziers, siphoning off not only the commerce but also the life from the dense, older, commercial heart of Beziers. In the Halles, the vendors struggle to provide a quality service to a population in transition. Probably, the best part of this Halles is its central location in the town and the great restaurants surrounding it. The highlight of a visit to Beziers is to plan one's visit to conclude with lunch in a local restaurant, particularly one bathed in the sunshine on a cool December day.

We headed to Beziers centre ville to check out the Halles, concerned that it may not be there next year. After purchasing a few items, we found ourselves on the north side of the building and in front of an interesting looking restaurant. The sun was bathing the terrace in full sunshine, people were putting on sunglasses and taking off jackets. This was the place for us! The menu was inventive and inexpensive. After making our choices, we were surprised to be asked by the elderly gentleman sitting behind us if we were from America. Mr. Smith had lived in Beziers for over thirty years and came every day to lunch at this restaurant. He enjoyed finding opportunities to speak English and to share stories of life in the heart of the city. He explained that at the turn of the last century, as the result of the important wine industry in this part of Languedoc, Beziers was the sixth largest city in France and was considered a cultural gem. Today, she has fallen on hard times although efforts to restore the centre ville are showing promise.

What we didn't learn until much later was the Mr. Smith himself had been a famous choir conductor and had only recently retired due to ill health. This quiet, unassuming man had opened our eyes to the beauty that lay around us.

It is interesting to use a visit to les Halles as a way to understand the local population. After the numerous meat stalls in Toulouse, Sete was a welcome change. Home to the largest oyster beds in France and an active fishing industry, Sete supplies endless amounts of fish and seafood to the rest of the country. It's no surprise to see numerous seafood stalls in les Halles. Much like the fruit and vegetable stalls, the fish are laid out on ice beds for the buyers to inspect. Again, such a different way of buying fish. We quietly stood back and watched the knowledgeable older women inspect the various fish and ask the vendor pointed questions before making their selections. Of all the markets that we visit in December, the Sete market, with numerous fish stalls was the most enlightening: nothing is in packaging, there is no "fishy" smell, the selection is enormous and the vendor will patiently explain the best way to prepare each fish. We walked around, checking out the various possibilities and asking questions and soliciting recipes from the vendors. As we moved beyond the seafood area, we came upon a fruit and vegetable vendor who clearly took great pride in displaying his wares. The overall effect was like a work of art with produce displayed to such advantage, using colour and texture to draw people closer.

One of our best market experiences was at Les Halles in Agde where we were shopping for meat and produce. Friends had recommended the butcher who sold lamb and mutton and off we went to make our purchases for the evening's dinner. After helping us select the best cuts for our proposed recipes, he asked if we had ever eaten *rognons blanc* (lamb testicles). Not only had we never eaten them, we did not imagine that they were something that we would want to try! However, after much encouragement, he offered us some as a small gift. He selected two rognons, each about the size of a golf ball and proceeded to carefully peel them much as one would peel an orange. He then instructed us to slice them thinly and sauté them gently in olive oil and garlic. That evening, after several glasses of wine, we carried out his instructions and enjoyed a simple delicacy found throughout much of France. Monique's reaction when I told her of our new taste test? She brought her fingers to her lips in that quintessential French way and said "Voila, ils sont exceptionals" (They are exceptional). Taking the risk in these culinary adventures is part of the thrill of visiting Languedoc. One word of caution, *rognons* on the menu may mean lamb kidneys.

There are still many Halles to visit and it is a delightful December morning adventure. We check the local specialties not found in the chain stores, it's a chance to practice French while learning more about the local customs and food preferences of each community and it's a great people-watching opportunity.

While Les Halles buildings continue to be the centre of market life in the larger towns and cities of Languedoc, their use as markets has all but disappeared in the small towns and villages. In our town, the former Halles, situated across from the church, is now the Mairie, its ground floor arches are closed in and the space is divided into offices for the local town hall. Just as in former years, it was the meeting place for daily interactions so too, today, it is the place where one goes to complete most of life's important transactions from finding a parking spot to getting registered in the community to complaining about the late night noise in the street. Life goes on much as it has through the centuries with these grand buildings and their arched doorways being a cornerstone to community life.

∞

The geography of Languedoc starts with the Pyrenées in the departments of Pyrenee-Oricntales and Ardeche and slowly edging down to the foothills of the Aude and Herault before they rise again up to the Montagne Noire and the Cevennes in Lozere and Gard. While the plains of the Aude and Herault are flat, they are also dotted with the cones of extinct volcanoes. These provided early inhabitants with natural fortifications and most of them are the site of *circulade* (circular) towns. Building started centuries ago on the pinnacle of the hill and over successive waves of development corkscrewed their way down and around the hill. These circulade fortified towns are only found in Languedoc and provide a ready-made opportunity to explore on the cool days of December.

> The sign on the outskirts of the village said "Circulade, 2000 ans". We wondered what the sign meant as we approached the village. We soon found ourselves heading up narrow, one way streets moving ever higher until we came to an open space on the top beside an ancient church. The café opposite the church offered a

chance to sit in the warm afternoon sun as we tried to figure out how we would find our way out of the village. As is often the case throughout France, the Mairie is the "go to" place for all questions regarding village life. We asked what the sign, Circulade, meant and were presented with a walking map showing the old town and the significance of the various buildings. Using the map as a guide, we spent a delightful hour twisting and turning through ever-smaller streets, peering and pointing at worn steps, arches and windows. The booklet explained how the first known settlers were retired Roman soldiers who were given land in Languedoc as a way of providing a military presence to keep the peace among marauding tribes. The booklet even directed us to houses where remnants of Roman architecture still existed. As we moved though the streets, we were directed to check out variations in street levels where new houses were built on the foundations of previous buildings. At one point, the booklet indicated that at a certain house, the foundations went down three stories as houses were built upon houses.

Even the design of the streets with their tight curves and blind alleys were remnants of attempts to protect themselves from enemies-horses could not easily navigate the tiny streets, ambush was easy from unseen corners, hidden doorways offered easy escape from the enemy. When we mentioned our recent walk to Monique, she explained that these same, ancient escapes were used as recently as WWII to allow the members of the Resistance to hide and escape.

After visiting Magalas, I went to our Mairie and asked if our village had any information as it was noted as a circulade town. I was handed a booklet that had been developed by the local history group and guided by the wooden numbers located on some of the buildings, we took ourselves on a historical tour of our village. We learned that a certain window in one street bore the hallmark of the style of the Bogomils, the sect that came from Bulgaria and preceded the Cathar theology. Entering an old vault, we learned that by looking down, we could see the foundation of a wall that had been identified as Roman. The booklet told us that around one tiny, tight corner in the street, was the birthplace of Charles Reboul, a resistance hero. The booklet had even been designed to lead us back to the bar in the Place where we could relax after our history lesson.

Soon, we were seeing the circulade sign outside several local villages and realized that this southern plain of the Herault provided its own unique geography and history. While not in any tourist guidebook, this hidden part of Languedoc offers the interested visitor the chance to explore during the quiet days of early December.

∞

While December offers lots of opportunity to create an interesting and informative visit to Languedoc, it's also a lovely time to enjoy the quiet pace before the Christmas season. There is nothing more relaxing than heading to the bar on a sunny afternoon and sitting on the enclosed outside terrace with a book and sunglasses. There is no problem nursing your coffee for as long as you want –the table is yours and no one will bother you and suggest it's time to order another one or move along. It's part of what makes life here so pleasant, adjusting to the pace, taking advantage of life's small pleasures and learning to appreciate the moment.

∞

The Marché de Noel or Christmas markets can start in early December but the main ones happen the last two weekends before Christmas. They are a recent introduction into life in Languedoc and are more typical of eastern France and Germany. The main features of the markets here are the food stalls and the selling of Santons. The selection of carved or clay Nativity figures continues to evole as they depict life in Languedoc over the generations. They now feature every sort of character or job that has existed in village life, past to present. These figures are handed down through families and new ones are added to expanding collections. Monique purchases one new santon per year and creates an elaborate village scene with the focal point being the nativity. However, the cradle is always left empty until December 25th after midnight mass and the wise men don't appear until January 6th.

∞

Another feature of the Christmas season are the extensive village decorations. They appear overnight and change the darkened streets into fairylands of colour and light. Each village seems to try and outdo the other.

> It was almost the middle of December before the village decorations appeared. The main street leading to the Mairie and church was strung overhead with garlands of blue and white lights cascading down making us think of melting icicles. It looks as though our village might win the contest for the best decorated village as the lights outshone all the neighbouring villages, brightening up the dark streets leading up to the church.

∞

In addition to the Marché de Noel, there are no end of Christmas concerts to attend. From traditional carol singing to orchestras and full choirs, the array is as varied as is the caliber of the performance.

We headed out on Sunday to attend the late afternoon performance of a choir that had a good reputation and promised to offer an interesting repertoire. As it was a glorious sunny afternoon, we decided to arrive in the village early and walk out into the countryside. We headed out along the well-marked trail and climbed up into the garrigue. I cut wild rosemary, bay and thyme to make a traditional Languedoc-style wreath for our front door. As we headed back down, we came across an elderly woman who was clearly distressed. In her rapid French, we understood her to say that she had lost her car keys as she was trying to round up her two little dogs. The three of us searched high and low in the nearby scrub, the car and the surrounding woods. To no avail. We suggested she call her family but she was reluctant to do this so we persevered in our search. By this time, the village bells were ringing to call us to the choir service. After several more minutes of increased anxiety on all our parts, she had this sudden look of surprise and reached down into her rather amble bosom and extracted her keys. We all hugged and with many thanks, she sent us on our way. We arrived just in time to hear wonderful music in the old church.

Andrea Swan with Monique Guezel

However, the highlight of the afternoon was our chance encounter with madam and her keys.

∞

As you walk through the village, it becomes clearer that Christmas is coming. French children leave out shoes under the Christmas tree to receive their gifts from Père Noel who arrives through a window rather than down the chimney. This explains the weird looking red-robed puppets lashed to balconies and window frames. Small pine trees and Christmas decorations are now sold at the regular Saturday markct; the turkeys, capons, geese and ducks hang by their beaks in the butchers' window awaiting prospective buyers; the bakeries and patisseries feature an array of *buche de Noel* (Yule Logs) to tempt the palate.

> We were asked to provide the buche de Noel for the Christmas feast we were invited to attend. We visited each patisserie to make our selection. The decision was difficult: at Katrine's, her husband had prepared mousse-filled yule logs covered in exquisite glistening icings and decorated with silver and gold balls; at M. Sabatier's, they featured rolled pound cakes drenched in liqueurs and covered with dried fruits and chocolate; at Mme Martin's, the yule cakes were rich, buttery cream confections covered in exotic flavoured icings such as grenadine, mango and nougat. How do we choose? Why didn't we offer to bring the wine?

The family Christmas meal is traditionally served on the evening of the 24th of December and is a marathon event usually broken by attendance at midnight Mass. Even in a country as secular as France, there are some customs that have not died out and the Christmas Reveillon is one of them. While the normal main French meal is often 2 hours long, these festive meals can easily run for more than 6 hours. Having an excuse to push away from the table and walk up the hill to the local church is greatly appreciated by the person and their liver and stomach.

When our neighbour, Simone invited us to join her family for Christmas Reveillon dinner, she suggested we come for 8PM. We wondered how we would ever stay awake until midnight which was several hours past our usual bedtime. The evening started with all the children and newest grandchild arriving at Mami et Papi's for the Christmas meal. We were 18 à table with even the youngest participating. There are typically no children's meal tables in France, everyone eat together. The meal began with platters of seafood, including oysters, mussels, clams and shrimp. The beverage of choice was champagne and it flowed freely and frequently. This was followed by foie gras with pain d'epices and various other breads and accompaniments. The local white wine provided an amusing pairing. By the end of these courses, we had met all the family and felt completely at home.

It was now 10PM and time for the main courses. The evening was still going strong, conversation still sounded lively and the children were showing no signs of flagging. Simone had prepared a turkey with chestnut and dried fruit dressing, a crispy potato dish and a variety of vegetable dishes. Unlike some dinners in North America, I noticed that portions were small and people took small bites and ate slowly. It didn't take long to adopt this pattern otherwise, we would have quickly needed bigger waistbands. The wine for this course came from the vineyard of Simone's brother just as the turkey and vegetables had come for her father's farm. The time passed quickly and it was soon the hour to depart for the church. We all bundled up against the cold, unheated church that awaited us and trudged up the hill joining with other families along the way. By the time we entered the church, our little troupe was now a rather large delegation and I'm sure it surprised the priest and had him wondering where all these stray souls had come from.

The candle light service in the cold, Romanesque church was inspiring, even for non-believers. We greeted each other with handshakes and bisous. There was an evident joy in being together with family and friends. The children were called to the front around the *crèche* (crib) and guided in singing to "bébé Jesus". At the end of the service, people quietly filed out, probably remembering that there was still cheese, dessert and coffee to get through.

Returning to Simone's, we settled back at the table following our excursion and tucked into the cheese course, supported by a hearty red wine that helped us forget the previous three hours of eating. I'm not sure how French children do it but except for the baby, all the others participated in the rest of the evening and there was no evidence of fussiness or discontent.

Now for the test-had we picked the correct buche de Noel in choosing the mousse buche? Fortunately, along with the traditional buche, Simone also served the *treize desserts*, a large tray laden with dried fruits, nuts and breads. It that is said to represent Jesus and the apostles. It contains "the four beggars" of raisins, walnuts, dried figs and almonds; olive bread with a selection of jams; quince paste, fresh fruits and sweets such as marzipan, anise biscuits, pain d'épice, oriellettes and calisson d'Aix.

The mousse buche was a perfect accompaniment with the dried fruits and breads. After all, it's mainly air isn't it? At least that's what we told ourselves. Everyone exclaimed that the ice wine we had brought from Canada was the perfect wine for these delicacies of Languedoc. We started to flag by 2:30 AM when Michel, Simone's husband, brought out the *digestifs* (non-fruit liqueurs) to settle our stomachs and accent the coffee. This led to another hour of quiet conversation before we realized that the family members were dwindling in number. The children had all quietly toddled off to bed along with the younger parents. Only the "old ones" continued the stories and reminiscences of Christmases past and hopes for the future. Finally, as the only ones who would head to another house, we said our goodbyes and thanked Simone and Michel for including us in this *Gros Souper* of Languedoc. Fortunately, the Christmas Day tradition is to recuperate from the excesses of the night before and enjoy quiet time with family.

In Monique's family, she gathers with her brothers and families to celebrate the Christmas traditions. She explained that their custom is to share the preparations and she sometimes provides a small sanglier for her contribution. As Pierre is from Brittany, they may prepare a Trou Normand for a course. Otherwise, the meal follows traditional Languedoc customs. We are not sure how easy it is to make some of these recipes in North America so perhaps they may form part of a French visit for you.

In choosing the recipes for December, Monique suggested that it would be best to present a few of the special treats that could add interest and some Languedoc authenticity to a North American Christmas feast.

TROU NORMAND

One of the best foods in France is ice cream. A quick check of any supermarket reveals an unending variety of delicious flavours and taste sensations. In addition to the ice creams, there are the wonderful sorbets and gelatos to check out. The Christmas meal is an ideal time to include a sorbet in the array of dishes served over the course of many hours. The idea of a Trou Normand is that the sorbet and apple liqueur (Calvados) from Normandy open up a *trou* (hole) in your stomach to provide space for the next main courses, aids in digestion and whets the appetite for the marathon ahead. While one could make the sorbet from scratch, the purchased ones are excellent. The trick to serving is to make a hole in the center of a scope of apple sorbet and pour in Calvados.

TROU LANGUEDOCIENE

For a Languedoc variation, Monique suggests using lemon sorbet drizzled with a fruit liqueur such as cherry, cassis or peach.

PATE DE COING
(QUINCE PASTE)

Now that quince are appearing on the trees and in the markets, it is time to prepare the quince paste for Christmas. Quince are common in North America but not used very often because of their hard, woody flesh. They are in the apple family and looked similar to gnarled, Golden Delish apples. They will more likely be found at farmers markets or specialty markets. Much like a Christmas fruit cake, the quince paste is made in early December and allowed to breathe until Christmas when it will be used as one of the thirteen traditional Christmas desserts. My experience in making this delicacy is that one is wise to make a double batch as there is too much temptation to sample it before Christmas. This treat is known in Spain as Membrillo and is delicious served with Manchego cheese, although a strong cheddar is a lovely accompaniment as well.

Ingredients:

5 large quince

$\frac{1}{2}$ teaspoon ground cinnamon

$\frac{1}{4}$ teaspoon ground cardamom

$\frac{1}{4}$ teaspoon ground cloves

Sufficient sugar to add to the quince

Sufficient water to barely cover quince pieces

Juice of 1 small lemon

Preparation:

Some recipes call for peeling the quince but I have found that simply coring them unpeeled gives more flavour and less work. Quince are hard to peel so I'm glad that this works well. Cut the quince into large pieces and remove the core.

The key is to weigh the quince pieces and use ⅔ of the amount of sugar.

Place the quince in a pot over medium heat and add just enough water to cover slightly. Add the lemon juice at this time. Cooking time will depend on the ripeness of the quince but it can easily take 30-45 minutes to break down the quince so that it is soft enough to mash easily. Stir frequently and be sure that there is enough liquid to keep it from sticking.

Once it is soft, add the sugar and spices. I have not given specific amounts of spice as taste may vary. I typically add ¼-½ teaspoon of each of the spices listed above.

Here comes the fun part, continue cooking this mixture until it becomes thick and turns a deep bronze colour. As Monique says, maintain the heat so that the mixture 'plup, plup, plups" while it is cooking. Stir frequently to prevent it from sticking to the bottom of the pot. Once the mixture has reached a thick, darkened consistency, remove from heat and allow it to cool slightly. Pour or ladle the mixture into a non-stick pan or coat the pan with a light film of vegetable oil. Cover with baking paper and place in a cool place. The mixture will harden to a thick, jelly texture over the next several days. Turn the paste over every few days to allow the other side to dry and harden.

The finished paste can be cut in to various slices and is a delicious accompaniment to cheeses or sliced meats.

PAIN D'ÉPICE

Pain d'epice is a spice bread often sold at the markets during the Christmas markets and is another of those wonderful French recipes that relies so heavily on local ingredients. It is a dense, spice bread served during the Christmas season as an accompaniment to fois gras. Otherwise, it is excellent served with dried fruits or quince paste. This recipe came from a friend who learned it from her grandmother.

Ingredients for 1 loaf:

2 cups of flour

2 cups of honey-she used honey gathered from a local farmer where is bees spent the summer in hives among the wildflowers in the Montagne Noire.

¼ cup brown sugar

1 teaspoon of baking soda

1 cup of milk

⅓ cup candied orange peel

1 cup crushed almonds

1 teaspoon of cinnamon

1 teaspoon of anis

1 teaspoon of ginger

1 tablespoon of orange water (I used orange juice)

½ teaspoon salt

2 large pinches of quatres épices (mixture of 2 parts ground white pepper, 1 part ground ginger, 1 part ground nutmeg, 1 part ground cloves). I make it up in small batches and keep it for any recipe that calls for multiple spices.

Preparation:

Preheat oven to 350°F and butter a medium size loaf pan

Bring the milk to a gentle boil and add the honey, stirring until it is completely dissolved

Leave this mixture on the stove for 3 minutes at very low heat

In a mixing bowl, mix together the salt, flour, baking soda, brown sugar, spices, orange peel

Add the dry ingredients to the milk and honey mixture and combine until it is a smooth paste

Mix in the candied orange peel

Fold mixture into the loaf pan and spread out evenly. Score a line down the centre of the batter and sprinkle the crushed almonds over top

Bake for 1 hour and 15 minutes or until a knife inserted into the middle comes out clean. Let it cool completely before turning out onto a plate.

TREIZE DESSERTS

The thirteen desserts are a staple for the Reveillon of Christmas Eve in Languedoc. The number thirteen represents Jesus Christ and his apostles. Monique says that the choices vary widely not only between communities across Languedoc but also among families. The only constant is the number of choices. The selection of dried fruits and nuts represent the four beggars-the main religious wandering communities of the medieval ages-the Dominicans, the Carmelites, Augustinians and the Francisicans. Next come the fruits such as fresh oranges that are a sign of wealth, apples, pears or melons. Then the candies that usually include Callisons d'Aix-an almond paste and apricot diamond shaped delicacy from Aix en Provence, oriellettes- a deep fried light pastry sprinkled with sugared orange water, pain d'epices, the lovely rich spice bread and always, two kinds of nougat, symbolizing good and evil. The other standard item is pompe à l'huile. The first time I saw this mentioned, I assumed that for some reason that did not make sense to me, there was an olive oil pump included. Perhaps one sprayed the candies with olive oil. Monique explained that this was a bread made with olive oil and because it keeps well, is traditionally eaten as part of a meal by workers in the vineyards. With the treize desserts, it symbolizes the bread used at the Last Supper. Monique stressed that the loaf must be broken and not cut otherwise, a bankruptcy might occur in the new year.

Monique showed me how she displays the desserts and she always, as dictated by tradition, includes three candles in the display. The goodies will stay out for three days after Christmas Eve and the expectation is that people will sample all thirteen desserts.

Andrea Swan with Monique Guezel

EPILOGUE

We have now come to the end of our twelve month journey through Languedoc. Monique and I started this book with the premise that people want to experience Languedoc as travelers and not merely as sightseers. We have gathered together the events, the history, the stories and the foods that make this such an interesting and welcoming part of France. As the region becomes better known to travelers, we appreciate that changes will happen. For the moment, there is still much to uncover and experience that remains close to the Languedocienne way of life. We hope that our efforts in presenting this book as a monthly format will enable the reader to answer the question that began our journey, "When is the best time to visit Languedoc?"

For us, it has always been about finding "le temps retrouvé". Whether you have the chance to travel to Languedoc and experience life here for yourself or whether you do it as an armchair traveler, we hope that you too, "find time" to slow down and savour life.

Monique and Andrea

RECIPE INDEX

ANDREA SWAN AND MONIQUE GUEZEL

Authors Andrea Swan and Monique Guezel have more than forty years' knowledge of the Languedoc. After being asked countless times, "When is the best time to visit the Languedoc?" they decided to team up to answer that question. The result is *Travels in Languedoc: Secrets to a Memorable Visit*.

Andrea has owned a house in Monique's village and visited the Languedoc for more than ten years. She delights in going beyond the typical tourist attractions and immersing herself in everyday life to experience the region's riches to the fullest. Andrea and her husband, Andy, spend six months of the year in the Languedoc and the other six months in Victoria, British Columbia. She is fluent in French and enjoys travelling the region to do research and collect anecdotes to share with her family and friends.

With deep roots in the Languedoc, Monique provides the secrets that only the locals know. She proudly shares her knowledge and understanding of the region and culture, including her recipes for authentic dishes that are popular in the Languedoc.

Printed in Canada